Reality Orientation

Principles & Practice

Lorna Rimmer Dip.C.O.T., S.R.O.T.

WP

WINSLOW PRESS

First published in 1982
by Winslow Press
23 Horn Street, Winslow, Buckinghamshire MK 3AP
Reprinted 1984

© Winslow Press 1982

ISBN 0 86388 013 4

Printed by Redesign
9 London Lane, London E8 3PR.

Contents

PART I

PART II

Activities

PREFACE

Lorna Rimmer is an Occupational Therapist who, since qualifying in 1967, has worked primarily in the psychiatric field. Four years ago she moved to Bedford and prior to taking up her current post as Head of the Department of Occupational Therapy, Psychiatric Unit, Bedford General Hospital she was involved in the setting up of a new Psycho-Geriatric Day Hospital.

In her work, along with her colleagues, she used the Reality Orientation approach to the treatment of geriatric patients.

In this book she outlines this fresh and enthusiastic approach and dispels the myth that working with the elderly can be dull and unrewarding.

The text is divided into two main parts. The first gives a detailed description of the principles of Reality Orientation and a practical guide to its implementation. The second part outlines specific activities to be included in the Reality Orientation Programme.

PART I

1 Theory and Principles

Introduction

Today we are confronted by the problem of an ever increasing population of elderly people, many of whom lack the family and social support that could once be relied upon. As a result of this our hospitals and old people's homes are under great pressure to cope with the ever increasing demands made upon them. At present the demand for care for this section of the population is not being adequately met. The staff involved are fully stretched and recruitment is often difficult since this is seen by many as an unattractive field in which to work. There is often a hopeless and helpless attitude prevailing in wards full of elderly people. Staff toil in an endless round of dressing, washing, toileting and feeding those who have abandoned performing such tasks for themselves. There is little conversation as patients withdraw and settle into isolation. A large proportion of these patients have problems concerning memory loss, disorientation and confusion.

We need to be looking at new ways of treating these people and to take a positive approach to their problems. Reality Orientation is just such an approach. It provides a method of combating confusion, disorientation, and memory loss. It stimulates patients, encouraging them out of their withdrawal and on towards greater independence. It can elevate staff from the role of drudges into teachers and therapists and give them greater enthusiasm, involvement and satisfaction in their work.

What is Reality Orientation?

Reality Orientation is a method of treating confusion, disorientation and memory loss by stimulating patients into re-learning basic facts about themselves and their environment. It is a technique which has been in use in the U.S.A. for several years. It was first developed in the 1950's in Topeka, Kansas and refined in the 1960's at the V.A. Hospital in Tuscalousa, Alabama. This work is well documented and is included amongst references in the bibliography at the end of this book. [1]

Studies carried out in America and Britain have produced encouraging and valuable results. They show that Reality Orientation works and is more effective in achieving its aims than simply increased staff attention, change of environment or other group work of a social nature can be. [2]

There are two methods of practice:—

    (i)   24-hour Reality Orientation

    (ii) Classroom Reality Orientation

These are practised independently or together. The most effective method is to use Classroom R.O. in a 24-Hour R.O. setting, thus giving the patients the maximum opportunity to benefit.

(i)   24-Hour Reality Orientation

Throughout the day patients are given information which helps to orientate them. Staff tell them their names, where they are and what is going on around them (for example, when they are being dressed, taken to the toilet or passed in the corridor) and they do this in a friendly supportive way in order to reduce the anxiety so often felt by those who are confused and disorientated. The consistent and enthusiastic efforts of the staff stimulate patients and encourage them to respond.

The patients' environment too is geared to offer maximum stimulation and guidance. Labels and signs tell patients where they are and help direct them to where they want to go.

(ii) Classroom or Group Reality Orientation

Patients are assessed and selected into small groups of three to eight according to their level of confusion, disorientation and functioning. These groups meet daily with the same staff and in the same room. Sessions last up to 30 minutes, depending on the attention span of these patients.

At the start of each session introductions are made. Then basic information is given to the patients as in 24-Hour R.O. Information including the name of the hospital or centre and the date is written on an orientation board which is central to each session. Encouragement is given for the information on the board to be repeated when staff have pointed it out and read it, or for it to be read and copied into diaries, according to the level at which the group is working.

Other activities for the group are chosen to provide stimulation and opportunities for learning. They may include naming or describing objects or matching words and pictures. Every attempt is made to help patients achieve success in some form and to be praised and encouraged as a result. The session should end happily and in a relaxed way with an enjoyable social activity, such as singing, playing dominoes or drinking tea together.

Who can be helped by Reality Orientation?

Any person suffering from disorientation, confusion and memory loss can be helped by R.O. It does not matter whether these problems have developed gradually due to senile dementia or have been precipitated by head injury, major surgery or a dramatic change in personal circumstances (such as bereavement).

Patients on long-stay wards in institutions could benefit from this approach in terms of the prevention of social withdrawal and the building up of levels of functioning as well as maintaining contact with reality.

Any elderly people, especially those living on their own, could benefit from a form of R.O. The technique could work in a preventative way for them by keeping them stimulated, reminded of facts and motivated to continue achieving. Sessions could take place in day centres, social clubs or perhaps at home if staff and volunteer resources are sufficient.

How does Reality Orientation Work?

Reality Orientation helps to prevent patients from withdrawing socially and cutting themselves off from the reality around them. The constant stimulation offered will, hopefully, draw them out of isolation and encourage them to make social contacts and develop and maintain relationships.

Sensory deprivation is experienced by the elderly in particular. As their sense organs begin to fail and their mobility to decrease so their isolation increases. These people are exposed to less and less sensory stimulation even in the hospital setting. Studies with healthy volunteers show that loss of function results from this deprivation and it is presumed that the elderly will suffer proportionately more because of the limitations of failing sense organs. Therefore, the sensory stimulation of Reality Orientation will help patients back to optimum functioning.[3]

Evidence suggests that the helpless, hopeless and negative attitude often adopted by elderly patients is a result of failures that they have encountered earlier, for whatever reason.

When memory or bodily functions fail and start to cause problems, mistakes or accidents, the resultant sense of failure can cause patients to give up their attempts at trying to do anything very much at all. This lessening of effort and of taking risks can become more generalised so that perfectly good function becomes lost and forgotten through disuse. If the supportive, encouraging atmosphere created in Reality Orientation can inspire effort and the taking of risks, then these functions can be regained and put back into use, thereby helping to boost confidence and encourage further progress towards achieving maximum potential.

Reality Orientation may help the patient to discover compensatory ways of coping and functioning despite the presence of organic brain damage, whether this be due to injury or the progressive deteriotation of dementia. The continual stimulation that the patient is receiving, together with the effort he is encouraged and persuaded to make, prompts the development and use of alternative neurological pathways. Such compensatory mechanisms are well recognised as being responsible for some of the recovery of function following stroke.

Reality Orientation is compatible with a behavioural approach. It can indeed be looked upon as behavioural re-training of orientation. In this case patients are rewarded when they give correct well-orientated responses. The rewards are encouragement, praise, approval and increased self-esteem. More tangible rewards could be considered as appropriate, e.g. cups of tea, cigarettes, outings, sweets.

2 Staffing

The Team

A team approach is vital to the success of Reality Orientation. Consistency of approach is very important therefore everyone who has contact with the patients should know about the treatment and be encouraged to take their part. In this way the patient will receive more stimulation, opportunity and encouragement and will not be confused by conflicting approaches from different members of staff.

The team could therefore include:—

Doctors, nurses, occupational therapists, psychologists, physiotherapists, speech therapists, social workers, domestic staff, relatives, friends, volunteers, the chaplain, and any other regular visitors to the ward.

The Role of the Staff

Staff fulfil the roles of teachers, guides and friends. They supply orientating information to their patients and encourage its frequent use. Staff also provide stimulation and motivation, trying in every way they can to elicit response and aid learning. Their role also includes the rewarding of patients' efforts with encouragement and praise.

Staff involved in R.O. need enthusiasm, initiative, patience and perseverance. They should have no illusions about the difficulties that face them and their patients. The work is hard and repetitive. It is not easy to keep presenting the same information in many different ways without tiring of the process. Nevertheless, the maintenance of enthusiasm is vital to the success of the technique. Plenty of support should be offered to staff in order to help them maintain their efforts and work effectively in R.O. It is a good idea for staff to meet together to discuss their difficulties and have the opportunity to express how they feel about their work. They may need help in looking constructively at what they are doing, especially when patients who are slow to respond or are even deteriorating, cause them to doubt their capabilities and to feel that they are failing.

Extra support for staff in the initial stages will be required when they may feel self-conscious and foolish as they state seemingly obvious facts about time, date or environment within earshot of their colleagues. Any insensitivity on the part of others can cause inhibition and hinder R.O. from being practised effectively. It is very important that staff have a well-defined sense of purpose in relation to their work. This will help them to overcome their difficulties and feel a bond with team members who share this sense of purpose. The value of the mutual support engendered within the team should not be underestimated.

Staff will often find themselves acting as the sole verbal contributors, especially in early and low level R.O. groups and with withdrawn individuals. It can be quite exhausting to provide all the conversation and questions and many of the answers, too! Inventiveness, enthusiasm and energy are needed to fill the vacuum left in these situations.

Staff must ensure that they have sufficient correct and up-to-date information about their patients. Background knowledge is very important for effective R.O. since staff must supply facts to the patients and correct their mistakes. They must be sure of details such as where patients live, their age and family circumstances and recent events of importance to them.

The Role of Relatives and Friends

Relatives and friends can help tremendously if time is spent in explaining the method to them and asking for their co-operation. If their support and understanding can be gained then they can provide reinforcement and encouragement. Specific jobs can also be given to them. They can help by collecting photographs, pictures or cuttings concerning the patient, his family, past job, places of work, hobbies, interests, pets and so on. Any information compiled will help build up a picture and give ideas for likely points of enjoyment and stimulation of the patient concerned.

With day patients it is a good idea to consider the possibility of a notebook or diary which could pass between home and hospital. This book could be kept up-to-date with detailed information concerning the patient's activities and his progress together with news of any happenings involving him. These might come up in conversation or could be used to stimulate speech. It would be an asset to know, for example, that Harry really *did* see his grand-daughter last night or that his son really *did* take him to the pub for a treat, should these topics come up in conversation. Staff need to be forewarned of important family events, so as to be able to respond appropriately if the subject arises and to be able to encourage response from the patient. Anxieties can be brought out into the open and help or comfort given. Happiness and pride can be shared and expanded by being talked about.

It is important to gain an understanding of the life-style of day patients and a knowledge of what their current reality consists. Knowing who is the prime minister is for them less relevant that knowing on which days they get ready to go to the hospital, when meals-on-wheels come and where their pension book is kept. Getting the shopping, feeding the pet, or taking tablets regularly are their vital daily tasks.

Your Approach

It is necessary to be calm and unhurried in your approach in order to reduce patients' anxiety to a minimum and avoid putting too much pressure on them.

Ample opportunity needs to be given for a response to be made and any semblance of tension or searching should be avoided. Try not to daunt patients and render them less willing to risk making replies.

Every attempt should be made to establish eye contact when communicating. This will help gain and keep the attention of those with whom you are working. They need to feel your interest focused upon them and to know that they have your fullest attention. If you appear distracted or inattentive you will lose contact with your patient. His thoughts may wander and his motivation will be lost. Try to adopt a warm and smiling facial expression which can be clearly read as encouragement by your patients.

Consider gently touching your patients on the arm or taking them by the hand when drawing them into conversation. The added stimulation will possibly raise their attention and help you to keep it. (Some patients may find this unacceptable and will clearly indicate so. Others definitely enjoy the physical contact.)

Think about positioning yourself close to and more at the level of the patient to whom you are talking. Draw up a stool alongside them, kneel beside their chair or move your chair next to theirs.

You must be prepared to take whatever steps are necessary to ensure that your patients achieve some success. They need to feel the satisfaction of achievement and the rewards of success. These are basic ingredients of this method of treatment. Be prepared to say or read out the response you want and help the patient to repeat or give clues or leads which will carry the patient on into a correct reply. If actions, pictures, words or whispers will help, then use them liberally, especially in the early stages. Then you can offer plenty of encouragement, praise, positive reinforcement and reward.

Be sensitive to the embarrassment or frustration that may be experienced by patients. If patients feel any loss of dignity they may respond with anger, withdrawal or avoidance and become inaccessible. Therefore, be ready to change your approach or alter the material you are using as needs dictate. Move on quickly to an area of known success or enjoyment for the patient. Perhaps you can show how you value them and increase their self-esteem by involving them in helping someone else.

Do not allow group sessions to be interrupted. Be very firm about dissuading visitors or callers. Any intrusion will be likely to cause a break in concentration and loss of contact with patients.

Keep as up-to-date as possible with news of patients' home circumstances and families so that you are sensitive to their needs as a result. Avoid any new work if there is an increased risk of failure due to upsets at home. Remain alert to any backward steps which may come as a result of physical illness, unhappiness or any other problems that arise.

Use your knowledge of patients to settle them down in the Day Room or Sitting Room. Put together patients from the same village or part of town or those with past occupations or hobbies in common. Take into consideration hearing or speech problems, mannerisms or habits. A reasonably chatty person needs a neighbour to hear and respond to his or her conversation. Alternatively he or she could be placed to help stimulate a more withdrawn patient to interact.

Let your patients realise that you are interested in them in ways other than those to do with information and learning. Build up your relationship by showing concern for their welfare and happiness and by taking notice of them as individuals. How are they? Did they have a good lunch? Is the tummy upset better? Did their son call in last night? and so on. Remember to comment on appearance and the smartness, prettiness, colour of clothing.

Notice new clothes, hair-do's, a good shave, smiling faces, good manners. Show your interest and appreciation in any way that occurs to you and give the recipient an opportunity for a boost of morale as a result.

Remember that achievements will be small and probably slow in coming. Try to keep in perspective the enormity of the problems that you and your patients are tackling. Be happy about and full of praise for tiny areas of effort or success. Do not become despondent. (It might show and reduce your chances of success.) Review the situation and try to be realistic. With those suffering from dementia you need to recognise the success of maintaining existing levels of functioning, let alone improving on these. Do not take anything for granted but let yourself and your patient benefit from the recognition of any small amount of response and progress.

Tackle only simple steps and take them slowly, one at a time. Do not move on until sufficient confidence has been built up by repeated success.

Perhaps you may need to revise and sub-divide your original goals for some patients. For example, goal 1 — 'Learn your own name', seems basic enough but possibly it will have been a great achievement to a) gain eye contact, b) hold it briefly, c) gain response to name when spoken.

Help yourself and your colleages by recording patients' efforts, reviewing goals and sharing experiences and ideas to further your work. Possibly others can see progress more objectively and can encourage you and help boost waning morale.

Above all disregard rambling talk and disorientated responses. They should not receive the attention that rewards efforts of rational speech. All staff should deal in the same way with this or it will not be effective. There needs to be a clear advantage for the patient to attempt to be coherent. If smiles and nods are the response he achieves either way, then his motivation to make effort will be lost.

A firm but kindly approach by staff tempered with a matter-of-fact attitude helps patients towards independence. It is necessary to ensure that patients do not equate friendliness and interest with receiving help in everyday activities that they will need to manage for themselves, if they are to remain or become independent. This matter-of-fact approach will also help when patients' mistakes or rambling speech need to be corrected. Such problems should be dealt with immediately and without sign of condemnation. It is vital to let the patient know that you are pleased he made the effort, happy that he tried, but that the response was wrong. Help him by letting him know what would have been right and encourage him to repeat it in order to aid learning.

3 The Environment for 24-hour Reality Orientation

The objective of 24-Hour Reality Orientation is to provide an environment whereby the patient can receive the maximum benefit from all aspects of his surroundings. Thought should be given to creating as stimulating, yet comfortable and manageable, an environment as possible.

The chapter deals with some of the ways of achieving these objectives and aims to stimulate development of further ideas.

Decor and Furnishings

If the opportunity for redecoration arises, then bright, cheerful and stimulating colours should be chosen for day areas. Wallpaper will give a more homely effect if it is available.

Any furnishings that are not standard institution issue (and can be approved by the fire officer) will add to the informality and cosiness of the environment. Items such as occasional tables, stools, plant stands, pictures, lamps, cushions, table covers and ornaments could be considered.

The furniture should be arranged to facilitate grouping of patients. By being together in small groups, patients are encouraged to become more aware of each other and to interact. Chairs ranged along walls may make for ease of floor cleaning, access, and, perhaps, observation, but they are depressingly rigid and restrict contact to immediate neighbours only.

Signs and Labels

In 24-Hour R.O. the areas patients use should be considered in terms of helping reduce confusion and adding to information.

Clear signs should be used so that they can be frequently pointed out and read by patients, as well as acting as guides for them. The name of the hospital and ward should be displayed. Offices, dining-room and toilets should be labelled. The use of symbols alongside the written word will help clarify the meaning for some patients, but symbols should not replace the written word. Each time a patient encounters a label it can be read for him and he can repeat it so that there is visual and auditory stimulation. If the symbols stimulate an interest, help form an association or give an opportunity to get something right, then they are succeeding in their purpose.

Coloured lines along hand-rails and floors will give a track to be followed to find the way to the toilet, for example. However, too many such lines for several different purposes could prove confusing.

Name badges, clearly legible, should be worn by all patients and staff. The use of Christian names helps create a more informal atmosphere but it is important to discover whether their use is acceptable to elderly people in particular and care should be taken to maintain the individual's respect. The badges themselves must be large enough to be easily seen and read without too close inspection. (See next chapter on Equipment.)

Labels should be attached to coathooks and to personal possessions including clothing. A personalised clothing and laundry service at your hospital will help in this aspect of your work. It will encourage patients to take more interest in their appearance by involving them in choosing their clothes. They can benefit from a sense of possession and greater dignity. Patients can also be encouraged to undertake simple hand laundry if facilities are available. With labelled clothing a patient can extract his own from a heap when he recognises his name (if he cannot identify his own clothes). His clothes can be pointed out to him and response encouraged.

Meal Times

Signs including a clock face giving the times of meals can be displayed on notice boards and in the dining room.

Place-name cards could be put out on the table at meal-times to encourage recognition and identification and could act as a teaching aid for staff. They will also enable staff to use their knowledge of patients in deciding how best to organise seating arrangements for practical and/or social reasons.

The use of table cloths will brighten up meal times and add to informality. Small table decorations or occasional flowers (arranged by patients) will add further informality, stimulation and a focus of interest.

If any non-institution crockery is available, it will be a pleasant, homely addition. Small teapots would make it possible for groups of patients to have tea together informally. Hopefully, they would become used to serving each other.

The use of napkins should be encouraged in the development of tidy eating habits. Named napkin rings could also be used. Older ladies may like to wear their own aprons at meal times.

Confused patients may easily forget the use of cutlery and hesitate or make mistakes. It is no use calling across the dining room telling them to use their fork/knife/spoon if they have forgotten the word and no longer associate it with the object by their plate. A needy patient should be identified and repeatedly given the cutlery along with instructions, such as, 'Joe, here is your fork. Use your fork to eat with', as a member if staff guides his hand into action. If a patient needs feeding tell him what is going on – about his cutlery and his food. Encourage him to hold his cutlery too. It may take a long time for him to feel sufficiently encouraged to try for himself, but the time that will be saved in the future by him feeding himself is very great indeed.

If the hospital has a daily menu giving choices to be filled in, then patients should be involved in this even if their participation seems unlikely at first. With the patients in small groups the information from the menu can be presented and perhaps expanded with details and comments such as:—

'The stew is always good on cold days like today.'

'I expect the pudding will be a bit stodgy for you, Harriet.'

'I know apple pie is your favourite, Tom.'

'You're always ready for a meal, aren't you Harry, especially when it comes round to 12 o'clock and lunch time. Let's start with you.'

The group may start by responding to you and work on to respond to each other. They can be shown the written word on the menu sheet or it can be written up on the board and they can be encouraged to read it out. The menu could be copied out into notebooks and perhaps names could be signed regularly on the meal order slip.

Personal Space

Personal space should be provided for each patient around his bed and locker. (These, too, should be clearly labelled). Friends and relatives can be encouraged to bring in small items to help nurture in the patient a feeling of familiarity with and belonging to his area. There are obvious problems with items being lost, broken or collected up and hoarded by others. However, these items do not need to be valuable and if explanations are first given to relatives then no great problems should arise.

Such items could include:– handbag, compact, etc. wallet, photographs, toilet bag, plus contents, calendar, holiday mementos, small vase, potted plant, clock, small box for oddments such as hair-grips, cuff-links, tissues.

These are fairly obvious items but many patients, especially long-stay patients, lack them.

Additional Equipment

Try to make the environment as pleasant and interesting as possible. Add to stimulation by providing equipment to cater for and encourage general interests and activities, for example,

— current newspapers, and magazines, books and clocks, to provide information;

— items which add to the informality and homeliness of the environment — potted plants with a small watering can so that patients can take care of them, a budgerigar or other pet, fish tank, music (record-player, tape recorder, piano or radio) and dusters (some elderly patients love to potter as they did at home and feel useful);

— a variety of games — playing cards, dominoes, cribbage, draughts, Shove ha'penny, skittles and darts, (if the latter can be carefully positioned and supervised).

— a range of items to encourage self care and interest in appearance. These could include shoe cleaning equipment, manicure set, rollers and other items for hair care, clothes brush and a clothes mending kit — including a button box.

Notice Board

A large notice board on which is displayed current information about the hospital, ward, patients, staff and the outside environment can be centrally located to provide information, interest, stimulation and decoration. This notice board plays a key part in Classroom Reality Orientation and is therefore described in detail in the next chapter. However, if you are not running Classroom R.O. this idea can be incorporated into the general environment of the ward. In fact, available wall space may dictate its location and space may not be available in the specific room that Classroom R.O. takes place if there are many groups held concurrently in a variety of small side rooms.

4 The Equipment for Classroom Reality Orientation

Before embarking upon the regular meetings of Classroom R.O. careful preparations are required. Among these is the provision of basic equipment. Each item is listed below with necessary description.

Furniture

You will need a table to work at. A round one is best if you have a choice.

Chairs: easy chairs of the variety that patients normally use for relaxing and resting in are not recommended. Patients need to be reasonably comfortable but sitting up and able to work at the table, as well as move their arms and legs freely for some of the games. Slightly padded upright chairs are best.

You will need storage space and a further table to set out activities on. (A trolley would be useful for this purpose — preferably a normal domestic one.)

Reality Orientation Board

This is a small portable board, measuring approximately 80 cm by 60 cm. Here is an example of the sort of information which is entered on to it. The words written in italics are changed daily and the other information can be permanently printed on the board.

Ward 4, Weller Wing	
Bedford Hospital	
Bedford	
The day is	*Monday*
The month is	*July*
The date is	*5th*
The year is	*1982*
The weather is	*sunny and hot*
Today is	*John's birthday*

An example of the R.O. Board.

This board can be made of wood with groves 5 cm. apart to take cards 5 cm. high on which days, months and numbers are boldly printed — a series of these can be prepared beforehand. Have some blank cards available to insert in the 'Today is' slot. In here put information such as 'April Fool's day', 'election day', 'pancake day' or a member of the ward's birthday.

Alternatively this board can be in the form of a blackboard with the permanent information painted on, or a commercially produced 'Magiboard' which has magnetic letters.

Notice Board

This, as opposed to the R.O. Board, is a large permanently fixed board. It is approximately 1m. high and should run the length of a wall at eye level. On this board arrange an attractive display of stimulating material. Here are some suggestions of items that should be displayed.

- photographs of staff members, clearly labelled

- photographs of members of the R.O. group, clearly labelled

- photograph of the hospital (or a drawing or print)

- photographs taken in the ward, e.g. parties, visits, etc.

- pictures or newspaper cuttings, showing the locality

- a calendar, marking off the days

- seasonal pictures giving clues for the time of year (e.g. spring lambs, bulbs, Maypole, Easter eggs)

- Someone's birthday (when appropriate)

- local or national event for the day (if no R.O. Board is in use (e.g. Guy Fawkes, Election Day, Charge Nurse Johns' baby born)

— Current affairs section, headlines and pictures of major events of general interest and short articles

— Other items to include on a rotating basis are:— The Royal Family, Prime Minister, Health Education Posters.

Many of the items will always be relevant and not need changing but some will fail to serve their purpose unless staff are careful to keep them up-to-date. Remember to leave time to deal with the board and keep it attractive, stimulating and current.

Note: It might be worth investing in a protective covering of clear fablon or plastic so that flimsy items are kept safe and you need not worry if patients reach up and touch pictures or if they forget and want to try and take them down.

Clocks

A plain, clearly numbered functioning clock is required for time telling in the promotion of orientation to time. Also required is a clock or clock face with movable hands which can be deliberately altered. Try to avoid a too obviously childish teaching clock.

Calendars

Again two are required. The first should be a plain chart with clearly numbered squares on which the date can be marked off daily. (This could be commercially produced or drawn up monthly.) The second needs to be a calendar with attractive seasonal pictures which will provide added interest and will reinforce the time of year.

Daily Newspaper

This is to stimulate interest in current affairs. A conveniently sized tabloid with its pictorial 'chatty' content has been found to be most useful.

Name Badges

Each person in the group (staff and patients) requires a name badge. If you know your patients have poor sight then make the badges appropriately large. Commercially available badges are often too small to be seen without careful scrutiny. Also, the pins may be a little dangerous, so take these points into consideration when looking for badges.

When patients begin Reality Orientation, the use of card to make up large labels 4 cm. high and varying in length according to the length of the name, is recommended. If your printing is not very good then use a stencil. Badges can be fixed to the clothing with sticky tape just for the duration of the session. Patients can be given or can select their badges at the beginning of the session and they can be collected at the end. As patients progress badges need not be so very prominent.

Mirror

A full length mirror will help you in your attempts to encourage self-awareness, attention to self-care and pride in appearance. One mounted on the wall is ideal.

Scrapbooks

Each patient in the group will require his own scrapbook once he has passed the initial stage of Classroom R.O. These can be purchased at a stationary shop or made out of sugar paper. (The nature of these scrapbooks is described in Part II: Orientation to Person.)

General Stationery

A good supply of pencils, ball point and felt tip pens, note pads, scissors and glue, needs to be available at all times. Individuals in the higher level groups also need a diary or exercise book.

Visual Aids

These are for use in conjunction with several of the activities described in the second part of the book.

— Number Cards: clearly printed numbers — use stencils on cards approx. 10 cm. square. You need two sets of identical cards numbered 1 — 20.

— Alphabet Cards: clearly printed single letters on cards approx. 10 cm. square. You need two sets of identical cards lettered A — Z. (Alternatively use Lexicon or Kan-u-Go cards.)

— Picture Cards of Everyday Objects. Commercially produced ones are available and they are of excellent size and clarity. To make your own you will need cards approx. 12 cm. square. If you are able to draw well then do your own illustrations, if not, collect pictures from catalogues and magazines. You need two identical sets.

Make up a collection of everyday objects to match the picture cards. Try to get articles that the patients are used to handling. Here is a suggested basic list, which can be built on to:

Crockery, cutlery, brush and comb, toothbrush, soap, razor, towel, pen, pencil, book, glasses, handbag, purse, money, fruit, newspaper, sweets, shirt, dress, scissors, nail file.

Dice and Spinners

Buy or make a varied selection of these. They need to be large enough to be visible to all members of the group.

Dice can be made of foam or plywood padded with foam and covered with material or even strong card and should measure approximately 8 — 10 cm. Wooden blocks of about 3 — 5 cm. could also be made. Each dice should have a different set of markings. Apart from the usual dots have one with the numerals 1 — 6 written on it, another with higher numerals e.g. 7 — 12 written on each face, another with a different colour on each face, another with letters of the alphabet printed on it and finally one with money denominations marked on, e.g. 50p, £1, 10p.

Cardboard spinners could be used instead of or in conjunction with the dice. These need to be at least 20 cm. in diameter and made of stiff card. Cut the card into an hexagon and mark each of the six segments as described for dice. Pierce the centre of the card with a pencil or sharp piece of wood. A length of sticky tape wrapped around the stick below the card will prevent it from sliding down.

Another type of spinner can be made for word games. This spinner needs to be large (approx. 50 cm. square) and preferably made of wood. The spinner needs to be constructed similarly to the fair ground 'Pomagne Wheel' with a wooden pointer fixed to the middle of the board, with a bead or oiled nut between the pointer and the board to facilitate easy spinning. Make a plastic arrow head for one end of the pointer so that there can be no discrepancy over which segment the pointer has landed in. On the board itself draw a large circle and divide it into at least 24 segments. Label each segment with a letter of the alphabet — it is best to exclude X and Z, but if more segments are drawn common letters such as vowels, S and R can be repeated. It might be easier to draw the face of the spinner on a piece of paper first and then cut it out, stick it onto the board and varnish it.

Balls

A selection of various sized balls is required for the activities described in the second part of this book. They can be plastic football, beach ball, tennis balls, air balls (golf sized) and sponge balls.

Items to Enhance the Environment

These are items which will add to the comfort, informality and attraction of the room, e.g. cushions, flowers and ornaments.

Games

A collection of commercially produced games is required (full details are given in the section on games p. 149). They include bingo, dominoes, flounders and playing cards.

Other Equipment

Here are some other items of equipment which although not essentials would be very useful for occasional use:—

record player, tape recorder, piano, percussion instruments, kitchen equipment, tea and coffee making equipment (including electric kettle), song book and song sheets.

The items listed in this chapter are all basic equipment which you need before you start Classroom R.O. However, as you progress with your groups, you will probably build up a supply of other items of equipment to cater for their specific needs.

5 Classroom Reality Orientation

For Classroom R.O. it is necessary to organise patients and staff into classes or groups. To achieve this an assessment of the patient's level of functioning is necessary.

Assessment

An initial assessment of patients to be involved in classroom R.O. should be made in order to:—

— Establish their suitablity for R.O

— Select them into appropriately graded groups

— Formulate goals for them

— Ensure that subsequent progress can be monitored

It is a good idea to approach your Psychology Department for help in this area. The method of assessment should be discussed with all disciplines of staff involved in the R.O. programme. The requirement is to establish as simply as possible, the patient's levels of functioning in the following areas:—

(i)   Orientation: person/time/place

(ii)   Memory

(iii) Concentration

(iv) Information

(v)   Basic reading/writing/numeracy

(vi) Eyesight

(vii) Hearing

(viii) Speech

(ix) Mood

(x)   Behaviour

These levels may be established by means of a test questionnaire or from recorded observations from the members of the staff team or a combination of both.

Test Questionnaire

The length of the test and the time taken to administer it are important considerations. Patients who suffer from confusion, disorientation and memory loss are unlikely to be able to concentrate for long and will tire of the procedure if it is lengthy. In many cases they are unable to answer only two or three of the questions. By the end of a long test concentration wanes and performance is poor. These problems are well recognised and documented. However, one still encounters over-long and complicated assessments in use.

Ensure that questions are clear, simple and to the point. Keep them to a minimum.

A sample test is included for your guidance but many other examples have been published. 4/5

Administering the Assessment

A perfectly straightforward questionnaire can become a nightmare when you are dealing with a confused and disorientated person. Do not underestimate the difficulty of the task.

It is important for the patient to feel sufficiently at ease to give of his best but he needs to be controlled to keep to the point of the exercise. A few words may be needed to help allay his anxiety but do not allow conversation to develop around the questions. Keep the patient kindly, but firmly, to the point. There are those who will chat, change the subject or try to divert you in order to avoid admitting that they have forgotten, or do not know, the answer you seek. Your facial expression and manner should not change appreciably in response to right or wrong answers. Thank the patient for his reply and continue with the next question.

With some patients the degree of confusion and disorientation may fluctuate causing changes in level of performance. Nursing staff may report greater alertness at certain times of day or day-to-day changes in mood and behaviour. In these cases it would be helpful to assess the patient on more than one occasion, choosing different times of day. Scores can be compared and the mean of the two used for grading purposes.

Do not assess patients at the end of a day, just after a tiring physiotherapy session or after lunch when they would like to have forty winks. Consider their routine when chosing a good time.

Use a quiet room, preferably without a phone, where you can be sure that you will not be disturbed. There should be a minimum of distractions for your patients, too.

Introduce yourself to the patient and explain what you are going to do. Try and put the patient at ease by saying something appropriate along the following lines:—

'When people have suffered strokes they often feel confused and find they become forgetful. I'm going to ask you some questions to see how well you can remember things.'
or

'As they get older many people find they tend to forget things. I'd like to ask you some questions to see if you have any problems with your memory that I can help you with.'

You are now ready to proceed with the assessment but remember not to offer any help or prompting. You must gain a true picture of the patient's unaided efforts.

Reality Orientation Assessment

1. What is your name?

2. My name is . . . . I want you to remember that for me please and I will ask you for it later.

3. How old are you?

4. What town/city do you live in?

5. What is the name of this place?

6. What is the date today?

7. What time would you say it was now?

8. Who is our present Prime Minister?

9. What is happening in . . . . . (insert a simple question in connection with a recent major news event).

10. Will you count up to twenty for me please?

11. What does this say? Will you read it please.
    (Present patient with test card, as below.)

12. Will you write your name here, please?

13. What is my name? Can you remember it?

> A cup of tea, bread, butter and
> jam with cakes would suit me
> well thank you.

Reading Test Card

SCORING THE ASSESSMENT

Ring the appropriate score

Question | Score

1) 0/1

2) −/−

3) 0/1

4) 0/1

5) 0/1 − it is a hospital, home / 2 correct names & nature

6) 0/1 − year / 2 − month / 3 − day

7) 0/1 − within am/pm / 2 − within the hour

8) 0/1

9) 0/1 − if any correct information given

10) 0/1 − faltering, some error / 2 − correct & flowing

11) 0/1 − faltering, at least 5 words / 2 − correct & flowing

12) 0/1 − attempt made, unclear / 2 − legible and correct

13) 0/1 − part of name or near / 2 − full name correct

ANALYSIS OF THE ASSESSMENT

	Question Number	Maximum Score Possible
Orientation:		
Person	1	1
Place	4, 5	3
Time	6, 7	5
Memory	3, 13	3
Information/Memory	8, 9	2
Reading	11	2
Writing	12	2
Numeracy/Concentration	10	2
MAXIMUM TOTAL SCORE		20

Using the total that a patient scores it will be possible to allocate him to a group. These groups will function at different levels which are outlined in detail in the next chapter. The following is an indication of the appropriate levels for the scores attained.

	Total Score	
Level I	0 – 3	
II	4 – 7	
III	8 – 12	These groups are likely
IV	13 – 16	to benefit the most
V	17 – 20	from R.O.

Recorded Observations

A rating scale filled in as a result of observations made on the ward may provide a more realistic assessment. Certainly it is often found that patients' performance suffers with the anxiety that a 'test' situation can produce. Staff most in contact with the patient (usually the nursing staff) could be encouraged to record observations made during routine procedures when patients are unaware that assessment is taking place and are functioning at their usual level.

A sample rating scale is included for your guidance but other rating scales are in use.
4a/6

Rating Scale

Orientation:

Person	Usually knows and responds to name	2
	Sometimes knows and responds to name	1
	Does not know name, seldom responds to it	0
Place	Usually knows where he is	2
	Sometimes knows where he is	1
	Does not know where he is; thinks he is elsewhere	0
Time	Usually aware of time (meals, bedtime)	2
	Sometimes aware of time	1
	Has no apparent concept of time	0
Memory	Shows signs of remembering	2
	Sometimes shows signs of remembering	1
	Rarely shows signs of remembering	0

Concentration	Can concentrate long enough to join activities, read paper, etc.	2
	Usually unable to concentrate for more than 10 minutes	1
	Unable to concentrate or even stay in one place for more than a few minutes	0
Behaviour	Always acceptable to others	2
	Sometimes unacceptable to others	1
	Often unacceptable, disturbing, or offensive to others	0
Mood	Remains stable	2
	Sometimes labile/variable	1
	Usually extremely variable, inappropriate	0
Social Interaction	Successfully interacts with other patients and staff	2
	Makes some attempt to interact and sometimes responds to approaches	1
	Makes no attempt to interact and barely responds to approaches	0
Sight	Can see adequately (with glasses, if worn)	2
	Has difficulty in seeing	1
	Appears not to see/is blind	0
Hearing	Can hear adequately (with hearing aid if worn)	2
	Appears to hear loud voice or sounds only	1
	Appears not to hear/is deaf	0
Communication	Always able to make himself understood	2
	Sometimes has difficulty in making himself understood	1
	Cannot make himself understood	0
Speech	Always speaks coherently and clearly	2
	Is sometimes incoherent/unintelligible	1
	Speaks incorrectly, is unintelligible	0

Reading	Able to read normal text	2
	Able to read large print or simple text	1
	Cannot read	0
Writing	Able to write legibly	2
	Writes illegibly	1
	Unable to write	0

Independence:

Toileting	Independent	2
	Needs reminders	1
	Is incontinent	0
Feeding	Independent	2
	Requires occasional supervision/help	1
	Requires feeding	0
Dressing	Independent	2
	Requires supervision/occasional help	1
	Requires dressing	0
Personal Hygene	Independent	2
	Requires reminding/some help	1
	Requires washing/bathing	0
Mobility	Fully ambulant without aid	2
	Ambulant with aid	1
	Cannot walk without help	0

The rating scale will give you a general picture of your patient's capabilities and behaviour. Obviously, the higher his score the more able he is. If all the patients on a ward, in a nursing home or Day Hospital are to be grouped for Classroom R.O., then this scale could be used to help group them appropriately.

Selecting Patients into Groups for Classroom R.O.

Having established a grade for patients who are to be involved in R.O., you can now select them into groups of the appropriate level. In low level groups 3 or 4 patients are ample for two staff to manage. In a mid-level group 5 or 6 patients can be managed but a higher level can include up to 8 or even 10. Due consideration however should be given to the following factors as well.

It is important to ensure that patients are not placed in a group where they might be made to feel embarassed and incapable by others who are more able. Nor should they be allowed to feel degraded and possibly become hostile by being 'classed' with those who they see as less able than themselves. So great care must be taken to establish the best level at which to start a patient. In very difficult cases, such as where patients are so withdrawn or incommunicative that you can not adequately assess their ability, you will have to grade them according to their nil scoring on assessment. However, you should remain especially alert to any response elicited from them by the stimulation, enthusiasm and interaction of the group. The quality of their response may indicate a higher level of orientation and information better suited to a higher grade of group.

Those patients overtly making more effort may simply be more verbal or trying hard to 'cover up' for their deficiencies. Do not be diverted from the work at hand. Use all the tact, diplomacy or even 'humour' you can to get back to your goal without appearing to directly snub or 'cut off' these people. Do not allow them to take over from the quiet ones who have possibly taken in more than they will reveal. Certainly do not upgrade the verbose until there is hard evidence for doing so. They will help stimulate the quieter ones — even if only by annoying them!

When there are signs of progress or deterioration, regrading the patient should be considered despite the difficulty for them of settling with a new group. More able patients will lose interest if they are not extended. On the other hand, if the demands are too great for patients they will be unable to cope, feel discouraged and perhaps give up making effort. They will not achieve any success enabling you to praise and encourage them. They will lack the positive feedback needed in R.O. to help promote further attempts. Therefore be prepared to regrade patients in order to ensure that you are enabling them to achieve their best at a pace that is comfortable, but sufficiently challenging to meet their needs.

Every attempt should be made to ensure that 'down-grading' is not recognised as such by patients and that any feelings of failure are avoided. In a ward situation it is likely that staffing will restrict the number of R.O. groups that can be run. In this case it would be helpful to remember that the most severely confused and disorientated patients may benefit least from R.O. groups.[6] Therefore the work would most constructively be carried out with medium to high-rated patients.

When selecting patients for classroom R.O. the following problems may cause you to consider them as unsuitable:—

(a) Behavioral Problems

Patients whose behaviour is likely to disrupt sessions and affect the concentration of others should not be included. It is unfair to jeopardize the effectiveness of the programme for other participants by including those likely to cause too much disturbance.

(b) Deafness

Those who can not hear or will not use their hearing aids should not be included in groups. Much of the stimulation will be lost on them and communication problems are too great. Their needs would be best considered individually. When you have gained experience with R.O. you might focus on this problem and help include these people.

(c) Blindness or very poor sight

As with deaf people, those whose sight is affected will miss much of the stimulation. They also pose special teaching problems and need individual help. With experience you may consider ways of including these people.

(d) Speech Problems

Patients suffering from these difficulties may suffer embarrassment, frustration and anger when they can not provide the verbal response expected in R.O. Their problems of interaction may also cause them to retreat further into silence. Discuss with the Speech Therapist whether one of you might cover some of the work individually before trying a group situation.

(e) Physical Disabilities

Patients with physical problems should only be excluded if:—

— There is no way of positioning them comfortably in the group.

— They are in pain and unable therefore to concentrate and make effort.

— Equipment cannot be adapted for their use.

Try to create a balance in each group by avoiding the inclusion of more than one patient posing special problems. Try also to create a balance of personalities and behaviour, e.g. those who are outgoing or gregarious with those who are withdrawn or quiet.

Selecting Staff for Classroom Reality Orientation

Ideally, two members of staff should work together in a classroom R.O. group and their basic compatability will be an obvious asset. Where shift work is undertaken it might be necessary to allocate three members of staff to ensure that two will be available for every session. Such a system would also cope with staff holidays and sickness. Continuity of staff encourages an R.O. group to build up confidence and trust. Patients come to know what is expected of them and learn to respond to specific individuals. Once they have learned to respond and have gained confidence and motivation they will respond to others. Time must be allowed for relationships to build up and for the benefit of them to be appreciated.

When staff are to be selected from a team already working together (e.g. on a hospital ward) care must be taken to minimize any rivalry or friction that could occur. If the work load is particularly heavy then R.O. may seem a relatively attractive and light option in comparison with taking patients to the toilet, bathing them and making beds. It would be sad if difficulties arose that could affect staff morale and hinder team work.

It is often felt advisable to rotate staff round the different R.O. groups running concurrently. After a period of 3 — 6 months staff move on to a new group. This has the benefit of helping them to take a fresh look at their work and preventing them from becoming submerged and stale. It will sometimes encourage renewed efforts. A fresh and different approach brought to a group can revitalize it and bring about stimulating changes. With a new group staff are also able to avoid or deal more effectively with difficulties that may have arisen in the past group by applying their experience. There is also the added advantage of avoiding a situation in which staff feel that others have groups which are easier, more cooperative and more motivated than the one they are struggling with.

6 Running Classroom Reality Orientation Sessions

BASIC PRINCIPLES

There are basic principles applying to Classroom R.O. which those involved in this work should always bear in mind.

Timing

Try to arrange to work in the mornings when patients are rested, more alert and able to give of their best. Take into consideration the ward routine and any other treatment the patients may be receiving — especially physiotherapy after which they will be tired.

Be wary of overexciting patients in sessions or of allowing activities to go on for so long that interest wanes. Your ability to judge timing will improve with experience and knowledge of your patients. In the meantime it is important to remain flexible with your programme. Earmark items which can most easily be left out of the programme, if something has to be. But be prepared with extra activity if needed.

Balance

When planning a programme for each R.O. session ensure that the material selected provides a balance between the following: —

work and enjoyment

the familiar and the new

active and passive participation

verbal and non-verbal responses.

Plan also for a variety of stimuli.

Instructions

Ensure that the instructions you are going to give are not too complicated. Try to simplify them and write them down in step-by-step form. If you rely on memory alone you may make them unnecessarily complicated and risk repeating them in a slightly different way each time. In order to avoid confusion you must give the instructions one at a time, repeating if necessary in the same form and speaking clearly and slowly.

Practise breaking instructions down into easy stages and go through them until you are sure there is no room for improvement. It is remarkably easy to make assumptions such as, 'everyone knows or remembers. . . .', but what happens if they follow your instructions to the letter and do exactly what you say, no more, no less, without using any initiative or foreknowledge?

It is a good idea to have a written copy of instructions with you during the session for reference. You will inevitably be diverted by someone or need to offer special help or encouragement to some member of the group and you may find it hard to get back to the point where you left off. You could put instructions up on a board or large chart before the session and use them both for your own reference and as a guide for patients.

Equipment and Materials

Make sure you have all the equipment and materials that you will need. You can not leave the group once it has started and do not want to risk the patients' loss of concentration if you falter or hunt around for things. Gather together and lay out everything that you will need before the session starts.

— Check that the equipment and materials are large and clear enough for use by those with poor sight or by all members of the group at one time when held in front of them.

— Ensure that materials can be handled safely to add to sensory input and allow for curiosity.

— Take any physical difficulties into consideration and check that equipment and materials are suitable (grip, one-handedness, etc).

PRACTICAL GUIDELINES

Having assessed all the patients going to be involved in Classroom R.O. and selected them into the appropriate groups, each with its members of staff, you will have an idea of at which level your group will funtion.

Here are guidelines to help you run the groups. Not all groups will begin on Level 1 or even Level 2. Up-grade your group to the next level when they are functioning with ease at the selected level. Conversely, not all groups will be capable of achieving the upper levels and for them the continued treatment at a certain level will have its own therapeutic value. On occasions it may be necessary to down-grade a group.

Level I

1st session.

This session might only last 10 minutes or so. Until your patients can achieve some degree of comfort and ease in their new R.O. room and with their new staff they should not be expected to get much work done. Their attention span is limited and concentration will doubtless be poor. Relax with them and communicate an air of informality, friendliness and interest. Show your pleasure at the attendance of your patients, their appearance and any interest or response they show.

(a) Introduce yourself as you indicate your name badge. Say the names of each person in turn as you show them their name badges. Encourage patients to say or repeat their names after you.

(b) Try to stimulate your group by showing them around the room and allow them to explore as you point things out and attempt to gain their interest. Allow only a few minutes for this but be flexible according to the response shown.

(c) Tell the patients that you will be meeting with them each day and that you want to help them work on any memory problems they may have. Introduce them to friends and give them some interesting activities to enjoy.

2nd session

Repeat (a) introduction and encouragement of repetition of names by each in turn.

Do not repeat (b). If patients wander you will have difficulty in re-capturing their attention for the next part of the session.

Repeat (c). Your statement at the previous session explaining the purpose of meeting together.

(d) Play the *Ball Call* game (see Part II Orientation to Person page 82) in order to encourage active participation, recognition and reaction to name, interaction and co-ordination.

3rd and subsequent sessions

Repeat (a) and (c)

(d)   Change the activity to help your group enjoy themselves and look forward to coming. As soon as they have become settled and used to participation move on to Level II.

Level II

1st session

This session can last for 15 – 20 minutes.

(a)   Cover introductions with patients giving their own names with prompting and/or reference to badges if necessary.

(b)   Show patients the R.O. board and read out the information to them. Attract the attention of each of them in turn and help them to read or repeat the information from the board.

(c)   Follow this with a sing-song or other enjoyable activity which will stimulate and encourage participation as well as give pleasure.

2nd session

Repeat (a) and (b)

(c)   Give a different social activity.

3rd and subsequent sessions

Repeat (a), (b) and (c)   but as the patients become used to the introduction of the R.O. board (not necessarily mastering it) insert another activity of 'educational' value before the social activity. Use object recognition, matching (see Part II Object Recognition page 97).

As patients learn what is expected of them and become familiar with the basic routine you can demand more in terms of effort and concentration.

Continue in this way until patients are ready for Level III, i.e.

(i)   They respond to their name and remember it (at least sometimes).

(ii)   They can read from the R.O. board and will participate in the activities of the group.

Level III

1st session

Patients should be able to concentrate for 20 — 25 minutes.

(a)   Introductions

(b)   Read R.O. board.

(c)   Write names and addresses (those who can and copying if necessary)

(d) Use an activity for specific sensory stimulation to interest them (see Part II p.132).

(e) Social activity for enjoyment and reward of extra effort, e.g. *Bingo* (see Part 2 — Social Activities p.151).

2nd session

Repeat (a), (b) and (c).

(d) Use a different educational activity to help build up vocabulary and use of words as well as providing stimulation, e.g. looking for pictures to match words or writing practice.

(e) Social activity.

Subsequent sessions

Continue adding to the number of educational activities, as members' concentration improves, until patients are ready for Level IV, i.e.

(i) They know their own names and the names of some others in the group.

(ii) They give the information from the R.O. board and try to write (not necessarily successfully).

(iii) They join in all activities and give mainly correct responses without undue prompting.

Patients should not miss this stage even if they are quite capable and did well on assessment. They do not need to remain on it for long but will benefit from becoming used to the format of sessions and the expectations of staff. They can move on when they are comfortably and confidently contributing.

Level IV

1st session: 25 — 30 minutes.

(a) Patients greet each other independently and provide names.

(b) Patients read information from the R.O. board.

(c) Patients copy information from the board into diaries with help. (Among older patients especially, there are those whose ability to write is never good. It is pointless to pursue this skill if anxiety is provoked as a result. Time should be spent on other difficulties that the patient has. They could perhaps just concentrate on signing their names.)

(d) An educational activity with which they are already familiar. (Avoid further new material until they are used to the additional task of writing up the diaries.)

2nd session

Repeat (a), (b) and (c)

(d) A different but familiar educational activity should be chosen.

(e) A change of social activity.

Subsequent sessions

Repeat (a), (b) and (c)

(d) Vary the educational activity to provide reinforcement of vocabulary and use of words plus plenty of varied stimulation.

(e) Continue to alternate old favourites with any new social activities you can think of to match the interests and tastes of the members of your group.

Level V

Sessions can now last at least half an hour.

(a)   Greetings and introductions.

(b)   Any up to date information could be passed on and discussed.

(c)   The date could be noted and crossed off a wall calendar. Patients could take responsibility for keeping the R.O. board up-to-date. The newspaper could be referred to for the date and any major items of news.

(d)   Current affairs or local events of interest or importance could form the basis of a weekly discussion.

(e)   Patients could be encouraged to keep personal diaries for interest's and to record facts to aid memory. Using a diary could help patients to learn how to find information to reassure themselves if they forget basic facts such as birthdays, appointments and addresses. Many other facts could be added to suit individual needs and circumstances. For example, day patients could be helped to note days of attendance, laundry day, meals-on-wheels, etc. This will help increase self-respect and confidence. Patients are unabled to face up to the problem of poor memory and master it.

(f)   Quizzes and games could be used to help keep patients mentally alert. Social activities will encourage interaction. A friendly informal atmosphere will add to the enjoyment of these sessions and perhaps bring about more sharing and caring amongst the participants.

More responsibilities can gradually be given to patients that they become more actively involved. They could help by:—

—   Suggesting activities

—   Writing a programme for the sessions.

—   Making a note or record of what went on in the session.

—   Making and serving tea or coffee.

— Tidying up and washing up afterwards.

— Suggesting seasonal or other material to decorate the notice board and room.

— Remembering to bring in contributions.

— Keeping the notice board up-to-date.

— Organising an activity or game.

— Giving a short talk about themselves, an interest, hobby or favourite subject.

These suggestions are not in any significant order and many others could be thought about. They are ideas to build upon and adapt. Some patients will enjoy the satisfaction of being given a specific role and the responsibility of remembering to carry it out. Others may need encouragement to take part and support to see it through. Active participation will help keep patients in the 'here and now' and gain them acceptance by and appreciation from their fellow patients. Thanks, praise and positive feedback will be coming enthusiastically from the staff too!

7 Monitoring Progress

The initial assessment acts as a basis on which to work and can also be used to monitor progress. It can be repeated after a period of time and dated records kept to show any changes.

Observations should be recorded as soon as possible after each session while they are fresh in the mind. It is better to use a simple form of reporting — the ease and speed of use will encourage keeping up-to-date. A lengthy, detailed and elaborate system will easily fall by the wayside when staff are busy and under pressure.

You should take particular note of:—

- Orientation

- Concentration

- Social Interaction

- Participation

- Memory

and comment on mood or behaviour if different from usual.

A duplicated sheet for each patient that can be quickly ticked is probably best. It should also give you room for special comments if you need to make any. Chart A illustrates this method. It can also form the basis of a simple graph made by joining up the ticks with a coloured felt-tip pen. A month's sessions can be recorded on the chart and any variation, fluctuation or trends will show up. This charting is a useful visual aid to take to staff meetings.

You may want to work out a chart that gives categories more closely connected with the level of functioning of your specific R.O. Group, lessening the range of possibilities to suit the capacities of patients.

e.g. Orientation: Person   Knew name
                                   Required prompting
                                   Responded to name

Staff may prefer using their own words to describe what they have observed in R.O. classes.

A simple record sheet for daily comments could be made up on the lines of Chart B. Brief reports can be recorded under appropriate headings in a space provided for that day.

A more detailed record kept in diary form and giving daily comments would be excellent but rather time-consuming.

A fuller report could be made weekly or monthly by combining daily findings and observing trends. This report could be given at the ward round or patient review meeting and discussed by the team.

It is helpful to have a folder for each patient in which you can keep copies of assessments, records and reports along with other information and details relevant to your R.O. work with that person.

A

MONTHLY RECORD SHEET

PATIENT'S NAME .... GROUP .... DATE ....

	M	T	W	TH	F	M	T	W	TH	F	M	T	W	TH	F	M	T	W	TH	F
Orientation																				
Good																				
Some, unaided																				
Little, with prompting																				
None																				
Concentration																				
All of the session																				
Most of the session																				
Some, patchy																				
None																				
Interaction																				
Made active efforts to interact																				
Responded to others																				
Little response																				
None																				
Participation																				
Actively participated throughout																				
Participated most of the session																				
Joined in, with persuasion																				
Uncooperative																				
Memory																				
Always remembering																				
Usually remembering																				
Occasionally remembering																				
Not remembering at all																				

Comments:

B

NAME:

Chart A: R. O. RECORD SHEET

	Monday	Tuesday	Wednesday	Thursday	Friday
Orientation: Person					
Place					
Time					
Concentration					
Memory					
Perseverance					
Interaction					
Mood					
Behaviour					

8 Final Checklist

If you are about to embark on a Reality Orientation programme check you have taken the following steps:

☐ Done thorough background reading

☐ Visited other hospitals or units using R.O.

☐ Involved colleagues directly concerned with the treatment of potential R.O. patients
  e.g. by organising a seminar and inviting an experienced worker in the field.

☐ Obtained the active co-operation of your colleagues

☐ Found a suitable room (Classroom R.O.)

☐ Collected, made and purchased the necessary equipment

☐ Considered the ward environment, (planned ahead and had necessary changes carried out)

☐ Discussed selection of patients with colleagues

☐ Assessed and selected patients

☐ Involved other staff, relatives, visitors and other concerned people. (Sent out a written explanation of what you intend to do, invited them to an informal coffee and talk or held an open day or some other meeting to enlist help and support from the very beginning).

☐ Found out as much as you can about your patients. (Found out what might particularly interest them, their past jobs and hobbies, as well as their social, cultural and educational background.)

☐ Agreed on the form of record keeping, reporting progress charts, etc. to be used

☐ Divided patients and staff into groups

☐ Set goals

☐ Planned and prepared sessions

☐ Arranged support groups for staff

PART II
Activities

Introduction

The following section is designed to help you plan programmes for Classroom Reality Orientation sessions. The Activities are grouped under headings for ease of selection. By selecting activities from these different headings you will ensure variety and can provide extra material from a specific heading if reinforcement is needed in that area.

It is hoped that this section will prove a helpful resource and a basis for more ideas to further your work in R.O.

Activities are divided into the following categories:—

Orientation	Person
	Place
	Time
Information	Object Recognition
	Numeracy
The Senses	Touch
	Smell
	Sight
	Hearing
Practical Activities	
Physical Activities	Exercises
	Active Games
Memory Games	
Social Activities	Games and
	Quizzes

1 Orientation

PERSON

Always address patients by name and ensure that they know you are talking particularly to them by establishing eye contact and then referring to them by name.

Bring other patients into the conversation by naming them and addressing comments and questions to them.

Use names as often as possible when talking to your patients. Always introduce yourself and your patients at the beginning of a session. This can be done in terms of greetings and welcome.

Patients and staff should wear name badges (see Equipment p.32). These can be pointed out and referred to as a reminder for patients and staff alike. They will facilitate the correct and frequent use of names.

Personal possessions should be marked with the patient's name (handbag, comb, photos, glasses, clothes, etc).

A photo of each member of the group (clearly labelled) could be put up on the notice board to be admired and act as a reminder.

Encourage patients to write their names and identify themselves and their possessions. They could sign a register during the session, sign daily menu sheets, sign their R.O. work in diaries and so on.

Encourage them to look into the mirror and recognise themselves, accept themselves as they are.

A personal scrapbook which includes details of their family along with photographs will be a useful reference and hopefully a happy reminder for patients (see p.86).

Activities to encourage use of names and recognition of self

You will need to collect individual photographs of the patients in your group, also photographs of them in groups with other patients and staff or visitors.

1. Show the photographs to your group and encourage identification and recognition. With patients capable of very little verbal response tell them about the photographs. Make comments and ask questions which can be answered by a nod of agreement or a smile, e.g. 'Now where are you on this one Mary? . . . . pause for response . . . . if not forthcoming . . . . 'This is you isn't it, over here?'

2. You will need clear snap shots for this activity. Place individual photographs on the table in front of patients at random, include photos of staff.

    (a) Ask everyone to look at the photos and find their own.

    (b) Give each an envelope to put their photo in and write their name on it. If patients do not respond remain positive — 'This is yours isn't it, Sam? Over here, yes, look at this.' Encourage patients to hold and look at the photos and help them put them in their envelopes.

3. Ball Call

    You will need a soft ball or bean bag to throw. Patients sit in a circle. The leader calls the name of one of the group and throws the ball to them (establish eye-contact before throwing). They return the ball and so on.

    Variations

    (a) Make this more difficult by relying on patients' recognition of name. Leader avoids looking directly at the person whose name is called.

    (b) Leader throws the ball to the person of their choice. The catcher calls their own name as they catch, then throws the ball back to the leader.

    (c) Leader throws the ball to the person of their choice. Everyone calls out the name of the catcher who then throws the ball back to the leader.

(d)   Leader throws the ball to any member of the group calling their name at the same time. The catcher chooses who to throw the ball to next and is encouraged to call them by name as he does so.

(e)   Leader throws the ball to the person of their choice calling their name at the same time. The catcher is given the name of the person to whom they should next throw the ball. The leader calls the name of the next person who should receive the ball (leaders' names should be included.)

4.   Names in Song

Try to find songs which can be adapted to mention patients' names to gain their attention and draw them into the group or activity.

For example,

'Quarter master's stores'

There was Sam, Sam (Pete, David, Joe or John) in the stores (pub, ward, shop, band).
e.g. 'There was Sam, Sam, eating bread and jam (drinking, playing . . . .) in the quartermaster's stores.'

or, *Uncle Tom Cobley and all*

e.g. 'John Green, John Green, lend me your new car (hat, shoes).
I want to go to London town (local market, party, etc.) with . . . . (names of patients in the group).

There are also many songs with names mentioned in them. You may find your patients names appear in them or perhaps you can adapt or invent some yourself (see p.127).

5.   Self Portraits

Introduce an art session with able patients. You will need paper, pencils, paint, aprons (or overalls).

You might like to encourage self-survey in the mirror before painting begins. Encourage patients to think and talk about what they see in the mirror. Be prepared to support and assist them.

Staff should participate and produce their own portrait to encourage patients. Talk as you paint, keeping patients focussed on what they are doing. You may need to help with use of paint brushes and paint if this is an unfamiliar activity.

6. **Name Cards**

Make up flash cards with the names of each member of the group, including staff. They should be clearly printed, stencilled on cards 5 cm. high.

(a) Hold up each card in turn, reading them and gaining the attention of the owner. Encourage reading, repetition, recognition. Hand the cards to the patients or put them in front of each one. You can ask for them back later and thereby focus, once again, on each name and individual in turn.

(b) Place the name cards face up on the table at random. Encourage patients to find their own card.

(c) Place the name cards face down on the table. Encourage patients to turn them up and see how long it takes to move them around to find their own.

(d) Place small 'prizes' wrapped and labelled (one for each patient) in the centre of the table. Let each person identify and collect his own 'prize'.

(e) Place small wrapped and labelled parcels around the room. Help patients to move around the room until they find and identify their own parcel.

7. **Name Spelling**

(a) You will need letter cards for this (see Equipment). Give each patient the letters which will make up their name. If necessary have their name card nearby to help them. Encourage patients to assemble their names using the letter cards. Help them form the word, then read it and praise them.

(b) Make a heap of letters in the centre of the table, ensuring that there are sufficient to make up the names of all the group. Encourage patients to select the letters they need and make up their names.

(c) Go through the letter cards holding them up in turn and ask if anyone's name begins with the letter.
Collect up all the letters needed to make up all the patients' name. Place name cards in front of the patients. Go through the letter cards in turn. Patients claim any letters they need to make their name. (Usually several will be needed at a time, if you have an able group, work on a 'first called first served basis'. Otherwise give letters to all who request them in order to shorten and simplify the game). The first patient forming their name wins.

8. **Role Call**

When patients are aware of each other by name, increase their awareness of the other people with whom they have contact.

Ask the group to supply names for some of the following people they know:

A nurse on the ward

A patient on the ward

A doctor

A domestic

A charge nurse

A porter

A physiotherapist, speech therapist, occupational therapist

(Use your own headings to suit the group.)

Move on to:

A singer

A politician

A sports personality

Repeat as above, but select a letter that the names should begin with.

9.   **Personal Scrapbook**

Provide each patient with their own scrapbook.

You may like to make these or help patients make them using sheets of coloured sugar paper folded in half and sewn or laced together along the fold. Some pages of lined paper could be added for writing on or stick pieces of lined paper on to the sugar paper leaving space around it for illustrations, pictures, photos, postcards etc. to be stuck on. The cover can be decorated with collage work, stencil patterns, doyleys, potato prints, wall paper, etc. The patient's name should appear boldly on the front.

Contents of the scrap book might include:

(a)   Family tree with or without photos — naming immediate family members and clearly showing the patient and his relationship with these other members. Birth dates could be found out and added to help serve as a reminder for birthdays.

(b)   Recent family events could be chronicled to keep the patient up to date and serve as topics of interest for future conversations.

For example: — Niece Anna has married (include a photo)

— Baby born to grand-daughter Jane

— Brother George and wife gone on holiday to Spain (postcard included)

— Maud and Harry are moving house

— Grandson has passed 5 'O'-levels

(c)   Some details of the patient's past, such as jobs, pets, hobbies and achievements may both please and stimulate the patient. This is helpful in getting time into perspective. A patient can be taken through these events/interests and through them brought up-to-date in as positive a way as possible.

These scrapbooks can be used as a reference by patients and the familiarity of them will give pleasure. If they could sometimes be available at visiting time, then they will act as a helpful source of interest and conversation for relatives who will in turn be reinforcing the work done in Reality Orientation sessions. It may also inspire other ideas for inclusion in the books as well as possibly further photographs, cuttings, drawings and additions.

Leave space for patients to add pictures that please them or help them collect material on a specific subject that interests them. Indeed try to find a particular subject that they would respond to.

10. Other Activities

If a member of your group comes from another country make time to focus on this. There may be a member of staff known to the group who comes from abroad or from a different cultural background. Older people may not have travelled much but may perhaps have served in the forces abroad or may have relatives now living in foreign countries.

Make use of any of these links or of others provided by a current news items concerning a foreign country.

Collect up information and visual aids, souvenirs, music, food crops, whatever you can find to make a display and to stimulate all senses. For example:

(a) Posters, picture postcards, travel brochures and maps could be looked at, discussed, passed round or put up on a board for all the group to see.

(b) Recorded music, national songs, dances or special musical instruments from that country could be listened to, demonstrated or joined in with.

(c) Samples of crops, foods, sweets or drinks could be passed around and possibly sampled while being talked about and compared.

(d) Souvenirs can be handled. Perhaps items of national costume, especially easy ones like hats, could be tried on.

A less able group can be encouraged to participate and receive as much sensory input as possible, being stimulated by the variety. More able patients can gain from discussion, interaction and the interest of something new. Very able patients can be given more facts about the country, its customs, industries and natural products. They can learn new information or re-awaken previously learnt facts. They can make comparisons and draw parallels with their own country if you direct the discussion.

This session could be followed up with a quiz compiled from the information that was presented.

PLACE

Remind your patients where they are now. Give them clues about their surroundings. Try to reduce any anxiety or confusion they may suffer as a result of not knowing where they are. (See Chapter 3 on the Environment for comments about signs and labels and notice board for ideas.)

The R.O. board which is shown to patients daily will give the name of the hospital or unit. Refer to it in conversation and remind them of it, e.g.

'It's good to see you here at the Day Hospital today, Brian.'

'You've been coming to St. John's Hospital for six months Mary.'

'This ward is part of Bedford Hospital, isn't it Sam?'

'At Weller Wing we always meet at 10 o'clock in the morning.'

Always look out for new pictures or cuttings from local newspapers which give you a different focus and way of bringing 'place' into your sessions. Mark day patients' homes on a road map of the town and put it up on the notice board. With day patients, put more emphasis on the local community than on the hospital itself. Remind them where they live as well as where they spend some part of their day. A scrapbook (see Personal Scrapbook in section on Person p.86) will help you here. You can turn to a picture of the patient's home and talk about it.

Other sources of information or material concerning the locality are:

The Library: Here you will get advice about books with pictorial as well as written details about the area, information about the history, famous people, industries, traditions, etc. as well as about places of natural beauty, poems written or stories told.

The Tourist Information Office: Here you can find maps, brochures and information on places of interest, historical buildings, etc.

The County Archivist: If there is an Archivist he will have facts and possibly some coloured slides about local places of historical interest.

Local transport companies may be able to provide you with maps or posters.

If you can find any pictures or prints showing local places in years gone by, they will often stimulate interest and give rise to comment and conversation, e.g. What was where before the bombing or new roadworks, how a new estate has changed the view or what farmland has now been lost due to development.

Activities to encourage awareness of place

(a) Help your patients to make up a scrapbook showing local amenities, industries (where patients used to work), parks, famous buildings and landmarks, famous people and their inventions/achievements, etc.

(b) Talk about photos and pictures.

(c) Have a slide show.

(d) Quiz: Make up questions from the information you have gathered. Ask the questions and allow for discussion to ensue.

(e) Hospital Quiz: For this you will need photos of parts of the hospital that patients use, e.g. the ward, day room, dining room, R.O. room, Sister's office, the grounds, main entrance.

Use these to stimulate interest. Comment and discussion as well as recognition and awareness. Show them in turn and see who is first to name the location.

TIME

It is important to bring patients into the 'here and now' when they talk in a way that shows their disorientation in time. Remind them, with the help of a calendar, that it is now 1982 and that they are x years old, that they are grandmothers, or whatever their current role is, that they no longer live in West Street or whatever is appropriate. This needs to be done in a firm but kindly way and to be done consistently by those who have contact with the patient. Try to adopt a positive approach by bringing the patient to the present and reminding them of some aspect that you know gives them pleasure. Do not simply wash away their past without bringing in a pleasant feature of the present, e.g.

'You no longer live in West Street, Mabel. You live with your daughter in Glebe Road in Bedford. Those lovely little grand-daughters of yours live there too. I've heard so much about them.'

'You were born in 1903 Sybil. That makes you 79 not 53. You have grand-children of your own now. Shall we look at those delightful photos you have of your grand-children?'

'You are 80 now George, not 50. You don't have to get up early to go to work. No more of that slogging away and heavy work for you.'

Help your patients to become more aware of time. Try to have more than one clock to give you auditory as well as visual information and draw attention to time. Consider a chiming or cuckoo clock. If patients have time pieces of their own encourage use of them, remembering to ask them to compare with you and give you the time.

Times of meals, R.O. sessions, visiting, favourite TV programmes, etc. could be written up in the most appropriate place with accompanying marked clock faces drawn alongside.

Bring time into conversation, remark on it and draw attention to it in any way that you can devise, making it as natural a process as possible.

'It's 10 o'clock George, time for coffee. I'm always very ready for a coffee by 10 o'clock, aren't you?'

'Is it 10.30 already, Grace? Our meeting is at 10.30 so we will have to hurry if that clock is right.'

Point out the clock at the beginning of the session reminding everyone of the time you meet. At the end of the session, note the time again and let everyone know the time you will meet tomorrow.

'I'll see you at 10.30 again tomorrow morning as usual.'

Games to encourage use of clocks:

   (a)   Using a clock with adjustable hands, show it to the group and ask what time is shown.

   (b)   Time Bingo: Make up cards with clock faces on them. (The number of clock faces will depend on the capability and concentration of your group. Two or three may well be enough.) The clock faces should be marked with different times.

          Make up small cards with these same times written on them. Put the cards in a box and use them for calling by drawing them out at random.

          Play as bingo. Each patient has a card to study. Caller draws one of the small cards and reads out the time on it. The patient correctly recognising that time on his card is given the called card to cover the appropriate clock face with.

   (c)   Using adjustable clock: Set the clock at times of everyday activities, e.g. breakfast, lunch, R.O. session. Ask what happens at those times.

   (d)   Using adjustable clock: Encourage patients to set the clock themselves in response to a question, e.g. When do you have lunch? What is your favourite time of day? — Do not forget to enquire why!

The R.O. board used daily in sessions will make patients aware of the date and calendars hung on the notice board or used to decorate walls will help keep patients in touch with the passage of time and keep them up-to-date.

A large clear calendar could be drawn up and used to mark off the days regularly in R.O. sessions, acting as an extra reminder of the date.

The newspaper will give the date and can be left on the table for reference. Encourage patients to look for the date on it as well as using it to keep up-to-date with the day's news.

Focus on special days and remind everyone of the date on birthdays, national holidays, annual events, etc. Pictures, photos, cuttings, songs, flowers, cards or decorations may add to the occasion and provide a variety of stimuli to encourage response from patients. They may also revive memories which can be shared.

Remember to draw attention to the date, commenting appropriately.

'Isn't it cold for June', 'March already and we hardly seem to have had any winter.' 'January seems very dull after the Christmas celebrations.' 'Time to plant our bulbs already.'

Try to include some seasonal material in the R.O. room or to help decorate the ward. Focus on it in the first session that it is new. Then allow it to drop into the background referring to it later, pointing it out as a reminder and way of bringing the season to the notice of the group.

Collect flowers, fruits, leaves (and possibly samples of crops in a rural community), pictures of animals and birds, and of people dressed for the season or engaged in appropriate sports; scenes showing sun, rain, fog, snow or seasonal tasks gardening. You may find sayings, poems or music that add to themes. There may also be foodstuffs, e.g. Christmas pudding, pancakes, hot cross buns, strawberries and cream.

January	—	New Year resolutions	July	—	Holidays
February	—	Valentines	August	—	Bank Holiday, harvest
March	—	Wind, spring flowers	September	—	Autumn, back-to-school
April	—	Showers, Easter lambs	October	—	Hallowe'en
May	—	Flowers, blossom, Maypole	November	—	Guy Fawkes
June	—	Hay-making	December	—	Christmas

You will think of many others, too.

2 Information

OBJECT RECOGNITION

Naming Objects

This activity is used to increase vocabulary, add to information and provide stimulation. Ensure that you use objects with which patients will come into daily contact. Keep them within his current reality. Draw up a vocabulary list of such everyday objects and make a collection of some of the easier items. Make a collection of such items (see p.103). Make or buy cards clearly showing pictures of these everyday items.

Activities to encourage naming objects

1. Hold up one item in front of patients sitting in a circle. Focus attention on the item and ask what it is. With a very early group you might want to put the item in their hands to help gain full attention. Pass it around and talk about it, giving a description and discussing its use. Prompt or give a 'run in' to encourage someone to say the word. Try and ensure that each person repeats the word whilst focusing on the object.

    —   More able groups can all call out the name of the object and the activity can thus be speeded up. Further items can be added to the list.

    —   Individual patients can be encouraged to take a turn at naming the object.

2. Using picture cards this time, spread the cards on the table in front of the patients.

    Ask for them in turn:

    'Who can find the . . . .?'
    'Where is the . . . .?'
    'Mary will you give me the . . . . please.'

3. Use picture cards and matching flash cards:
    Spread the cards on the table again. Hold up a flash card. Encourage patients to read the card and find the picture to go with it.

4.   Spread out the flash cards. Hold up objects or cards in turn. Encourage patients to find the appropriate flash card to match what you are holding.

5.   Spread out picture cards. Give each patient one or two flash cards. See who can match theirs first.

Able patients can manage this quite quickly and the number of cards used can be increased by having more than one 'round'. Clear the table and set out further cards. The game can be speeded up by giving patients a further flash card as soon as they have placed the previous one.

Move on to naming objects beginning with a specific letter.

1.   Place cards or objects on the table. Ask 'What are they called?' 'Which begins with the letter B?' Until all objects are named.

2.   **I-Spy:**

'Can you name something in this room beginning with 'C'?' You could point or prompt if necessary.

3.   **Scavenger:** This game could involve patients moving around the room, if you wish. Otherwise provide objects close at hand. Place items around the room in easily accessible, obvious places. Ask 'Who can find me a book?' or 'Who can show me a pen?'

4.   **Magazine Hunt**

(Women's magazines give best variety of pictures). Distribute magazines. Ask patients to look and find a picture of: a baby, cigarette, book, chair, etc.

Encourage recognition of everyday objects by using matching games, bring in the use of words, too.

1. Using everyday object cards — have two sets for an exact match. Spread one set on the table. Hold up the others in turn and ask for its pair.

2. Make your own cards. Use magazine pictures, adverts, blocks of colour, anything you can think of and duplicate. The cards can be made increasingly smaller.

2(a). Put sets of pictures into large envelopes. There should be enough sets for patients each to have a set to sort out and put into pairs.

2(b). Give each person a set of cards to pair up and see who finishes first.

3. Make this activity more difficult by using pictures of the same object but a different design:

   e.g a china willow pattern teapot and a stainless steel teapot
   a Great Dane and an old English sheep dog.

4. Introduce greater difficulty and the need to form associations:

   e.g. car and plane — transport
   sausages and icecream — food
   knife and pan — made of metal.

   Use fewer cards per patient for this and encourage them to explain why they have paired them as they have. Alternatively, offer help and guidance.

   'Which ones could you eat?'

   'Which could you travel in?'

5(a). Have a collection of picture cards to act as clues for this game. Write a short word on the blackboard spelt with its letters running down the left-hand side. Choose an easy well-known word. Ask patients to give you words to fill in on the board. These words must each begin with the letters that made up the original work, e.g.

   C up
   H at
   A pple
   I ce-cream
   R ose

You will need to remind patients of the letter they are using and what they are trying to find. Talk and focus attention, prompt and help to ensure success.

5(b).Those patients who are more able could move on to finding words which all come from a similar grouping, e.g. Christian names, foodstuffs, flowers, countries.

It is a good idea to work some out before the session so that you can ensure only 'possible' words are chosen and can give clues and prompts when the going is hard.

Move on to naming objects beginning with a specific letter.

You will need letter cards, an alphabet pointer or a specially made 5 cm. dice with common letters printed on each face (See Equipment – Chapter 4 p.34).

1(a). Go through the shuffled alphabet cards to select a letter. Tell everyone the letter. Hold up the card and ask for a word which begins with it.

1(b).Patients throw the letter dice in turn, whichever letter they score, a word is found beginning with it.

2(a). Select a letter card, hold it up. Ask for a word from a particular group of nouns. e.g. a name, an animal, something to eat.

2(b).Write up a short list on the board
e.g. girl's name, boy's name, animal, town, fruit or vegetable, etc.
Select a letter by using pointer, dice or cards. Ask for items to make up the list.

2(c). Give out pencils and papers. Play as above but everyone writes down their answers. When finished go round the group asking in turn for their girl's name, then boy's name, etc. Patient scores 2 if no-one else has that answer or scores 1 if anyone else has the same answer.

2(d).Add to the items being searched for to make the game more difficult, e.g. fish, bird, river, sport, job or profession, items of clothing, beverage, country, famous person.

3.   **A – Z.**
You can play this as a group, writing answers on the board. Alternatively, hand out pencils and paper. Choose a subject from the list given in the previous game.

Find an item for each letter of the alphabet to suit that subject. How many can be found.

e.g. A – Z Fruit

Apple

Banana

Crab-apple

Damson

Elderberry

Fig

Grapefruit, etc.

Work out some answers beforehand so that you can give clues and prompts, keeping the game moving. You risk losing attention if too much time elapses and patients find the effort too great. Keep reminding them of the task and bring 'back in' any whose attention wanders.

(There are encyclopaedias, handbooks, Observer books and other guides which will supply you with answers).

4. **Magazine Hunt**

Distribute magazines. Select a letter, (using pointer, dice or going through letter words). Everyone searches through their magazine to find a picture of something beginning with that letter. Stop and write it up on the board when it is found in order to give everyone a breathing space. Write up the name of the person who found the picture. Move on to the next letter. Whoever finds the most items is the winner.

5. **The Use of Everyday Objects**

You will need everyday object picture cards, with patients sitting in a circle.

5(a). Show a card to a member of the group. Encourage them to act out (mime) the use of that object. Who can guess what they are using?
(Items to choose:– toothbrush, lipstick, razor, cup, spoon, comb, glasses, pen.)

5(b). Play as above but patients pick a card at random from a selection held out, upside down for them to choose.

5(c). Play as above but without cards. Patients choose own subjects to mime.

5(d). Give out pencils and paper. Staff mime use of five or ten everyday objects. Patients write down their answers.

Follow on from the use of everyday objects to the use of more complicated, less commonly encountered objects for those confined to hospital. Things they would see in shops, on the streets and on the television.

Sequences

More able patients should now be introduced to simple sequences. These patients will have difficulty with abstract thinking and forming associations. They become confused forgetting what the next step should be. They may loose concentration or confidence at any point in the process and give up trying.

Start by using picture cards which show cause and effect, e.g.

cup is knocked — tea spills out
person slips — and falls over
cigarette is dropped — a fire begins

Think of your own examples and try to illustrate them. Keep within the patients' present experience to start with. Move on to sequences required in everyday activities.

e.g. washing, shaving, getting a drink.

There are commercially produced cards for this purpose. Show the cards to your group. Talk about the actions portrayed. Arrange the cards in sequence seeking patients' approval as you do so. Collect them up, mix them, give them out and ask a patient to complete the task for you.

Alternatively give each patient a different sequence to arrange and then confer together when everyone has finished. You could bring into the R.O. room the equipment needed for patients to try out sequences.

EXAMPLES OF EVERYDAY OBJECTS

Food

fruit
cake
chocolate
sugar
biscuits
salt/pepper
sweets

Drink

beer
tea
water
coffee
orange squash

Hospital

doctor
medicine
nurse
ambulance

Personal Belongings

stick
make-up
glasses
watch
teeth
newspaper
money
cigarettes
book
Bible
brush & comb
handbag
pipe
pen & paper
hotwater bottle
radio

Toilet Items

tissues
toothbrush
bottle
soap
razor
bedpan
flannel
toilet

Furniture

rug
bed
cushion
chair

Clothes

cardigan
dress
hat
pyjamas
slippers
coat
gloves
dressing-gown
shirt
shoes
night-dress

Others

TV
car
telephone
light

NUMERACY

Encourage awareness and use of number in all activities. Remember to bring number into the conversation by commenting on it, e.g.

'There are 4 of us today — 1, 2, 3, 4.'

'It's the 5th of April today.'

Count up days marked off on the calendar *'1st, 2nd, 3rd, 4th, 5th.'*

'Here are 3 cards George' . . . . *'1, 2, 3.'*

You will need number cards (see equipment p.33), large and small dice, preferably two with numbers and two with dots (p.33).

SIMPLE NUMBER GAMES

1(a) **Using large dice**
Patients sit in circle. Each throws the dice in turn and calls the score to a staff member who writes it up on the blackboard, adding each patient's score as he goes. After an agreed number of turns or after a set time the highest score wins.

1(b) Play as above but the winner is the first to reach a score of, say, 50.

2. **Using Number Cards**
Distribute number cards to patients and staff sitting in a circle around a table. Leave the cards in front of the patients to remind them of their number. Throw the dice and call the number thrown. The person who has that number should see and hear it and be encouraged to respond by taking the dice. He throws the dice next.

The winner is the person whose number has come up the most times after an agreed number of turns or after a set time.

3. **Count items in the room.**

    Ask patients how many windows, chairs, people etc there are?

    Either give a different item for each patient to count in turn or ask at random.

4(a) **Items on a tray**

    Arrange small everyday items on a tray or on the table in front of patients. Place the items in groups, e.g.

    > 2 pairs of scissors
    >
    > 4 pencils
    >
    > 1 cup
    >
    > 5 spoons

    Ask 'How many . . . . . are there?'

4(b) Add or subtract items and ask again, 'How many?'

    Let patients add or subtract items to give the number you request.

4(c) Rearrange items at random and ask 'How many?'

5. **Dominoes** (ordinary commercially produced set, larger wooden one or card set marked with dots).

6. **Number dominoes**

    Make dominoes with clear numbers instead of dots. (These are also available commercially). Play as ordinary dominoes, matching number to number.

7. **Number Bingo**

(a) Simple version. You will need 2 sets of number cards. Give patients 2 or 3 number cards from one pack. Leader goes through the second pack calling each card in turn. When patients recognise the number being called as one of their numbers they turn that card over. (Staff could take called cards away to prevent confusion). The first person to have all their cards called wins.

(b) Ordinary, commercial Bingo or you could make your own larger cards with fewer numbers.

8. **Dice High Target**

Requirements:

1 large dice

6 bean bags or balls

Large box, tin or wastepaper basket.

Patients sit in a circle with the box in the centre. Each person throws the dice in turn. The score on the dice determines the number of balls a patient is given to throw into the box. A patient throwing a 5 on the dice is given five balls. He aims these at the box. The number landing in the box count as that patient's score.

Winner is the person who scores most in a set number of turns or after a set time.

9. **Prize Dice**

Requirements:

1 large dice

Selection of small prizes

A number between 1 and 6 is chosen. This number becomes the prize number. Patients sit in a circle. The dice is thrown in turn. Each time the prize number is thrown the thrower receives a small prize.

10 **Chequers**

For this you will need a large wooden board marked out as shown. (A paper one would do or one chalked out on the floor if you can manage to renew the chalk quickly enough). Squares should be marked out and scores written in the squares.

2	5	2
5	10	5
2	5	2

Squares need to be large enough to fit a small bean bag inside them (i.e. approx. 30 − 40 cm.)

You will need two bean bags or specially-made counters for this game, too.

Patients sit in a circle around the chequer board. Each patient has 2 bean bags to throw and if they land in a square they score. Those landing half-in half-out do not score. Encourage patients to call out and total their own scores for staff to write up on the blackboard.

11. **Pass the Parcel**
     Requirements:

> *A large dice*
> *Well-wrapped parcel*

Patients sit in a circle. The dice is thrown and the parcel moves round the number of people equivalent to the number thrown on the dice. Wherever the parcel stops the patient holding it undoes one layer of the wrapping paper. The dice is thrown again and the parcel moves on appropriately and so on until the parcel is unwrapped and claimed by the person taking off the final layer.

Decimal Coinage

For many long-stay patients money seems of little importance and they may feel they have no use for it. However, all patients have money and you can try to develop the basic skill required in dealing with it. You may be able to encourage use of the hospital shop for buying personal items. A visit to shops in the local town could be a highlight and act as a reward for hard work in R.O. sessions. If your patients can gain confidence in using money and dealing with it sensibly, they can be more involved in choosing their own clothes and possessions and in choosing small gifts for family and friends on special occasions.

For Day patients it is vital to their independence that they should be able to deal with their money. It is important too for their safety and dignity.

Sorting out coins to pay amounts under £1 and being sure of correct change are very common problems. People become anxious and feel flustered and foolish as they sort among their coins to find the correct money. Many patients abandon doing this and always pay with £1 notes, hoping for the correct change rather then risking embarrassment.

Even the more able Day patients may have difficulty dealing with coins and could benefit from help.

Simple activities to encourage use of decimal coins

Make cards with decimal coins printed on them; draw around coins to give correct size and copy the design onto the shape. For less able groups make up cards with only 2 or 3 coins on them, otherwise have the complete set of coins on one card. If possible provide real coins for use, otherwise buy plastic ones or cut cardboard shapes to size (but these are less satisfactory).

1(a) Give each patient a card. Supply coins for each patient to examine and select to match those on his card. Give each patient help and encouragement telling him about the coins and naming them.

1(b) More able patients can undertake this activity competatively by seeing who can fill their card up first.

1(c) Leader calls the coin to be found and fitted on the card. When everyone has that coin in place the next is called.

1(d) Each patient in turn picks a coin from a set in a bag which is handed to him. He names the coin. Everyone matches it and so on.

2. Give each patient a supply of coins. The leader asks for a specific coin. See who is the first to produce it.

You can keep score and award a prize. This can be a game of speed for able patients and of identification for less able patients.

Build up requests, asking for:

> *'A 2p and a 10p please'.*
> *'A 1p, 5p and 50p please'*, etc.

Build up further by requiring some arithmetic to be done:

> *'13p please'*
> *'21p, 37p'*
> *'£1. 02'*

3. **Dice**
Requirements: *dice printed with decimal coins*

3(a) With patients sitting in a circle. Use large 10 cm. dice to throw in turn. Thrower calls out 'score' to staff who totals it on the blackboard. Winner scores most in a set number of rounds or in a set time.

3(b) Set a target score, say, £1.10p. Play as above. Winner is the first to reach the target score or if necessary the person nearest to that sum.

3(c) Have a group target. See how long it takes to reach £5.

3(d) More able players can play as above but around a table using 5cm. dice. Each person can have pencil and paper to total their own score. To achieve target the exact coins must be thrown at the end. If the amount thrown is too high it does not count and play continues.

4. Play at the table using 5cm. dice. You will need coins for this game too. Each person throws the dice and calls the score. A coin of that value is given to the scorer. After a few rounds patients total up their coins to see who has the highest sum. (You could consider handing out £1 tokens to those who wish to 'cash-in' coins to make counting up easier.

5. **Bingo**

This game can be adapted to give simple and enjoyable coinage recognition practice for less able patients. Patients are given cards with 2 or 3 decimal coins marked on them. Each card has a different combination of coins depicted. The caller takes a coin or marked card from a bag and calls out which one it is. Patients finding that coin marked on their card cover it over or cross it out. The first person to have covered over or crossed out all the coins on their card calls Bingo and wins.

6. **Coin Man**

You will need a decimal dice for this game, coins, black board or pencils and paper. It can be played as a group with a member of staff drawing the man on a blackboard as he is scored or with each patient making up their own man with paper and pencil provided. Alternatively coins can be given out for each to make their own man.

Each person throws the dice in turn and the 50p must be thrown before play can begin in earnest.

50p scores a body (a subsequent 50p gives the player an extra throw of the dice.)

Once the body is in position a score of 10p gives a head, 2p each leg, 5p each arm, 1p each foot, ½p each hand.

COIN MAN

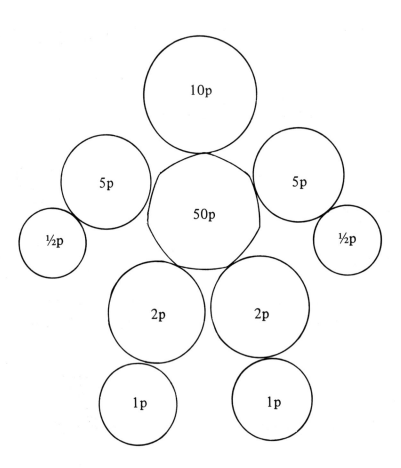

7. **Encourage patients to use the hospital shop**

Encourage awareness of prices, especially with Day Patients. Show your group items marked with price labels.

Plan shopping lists and let them suggest prices (see practical activities p.134).

TOUCH

In order to provide as much sensory input as possible encourage your patients to touch, as well as look at, the things around them. Remember to pass items around the group so that each can focus on them in turn. There is an added possibility of gaining attention and response when the patient can see an item, feel it and hear you talking about it. Remember this throughout all the activities you run with your group.

Activities to specifically encourage the use of touch and the recognition of forms

1. **Feely bag**

You will need a cushion cover, shoe bag, pillow case or specially made draw-string bag for this.

Collect a few unbreakable objects which have no sharp or pointed edges. Make sure they are objects in common usage with your patients, e.g. teaspoon, box of matches, comb, pencil.

Place an object in the bag.

Encourage patients to put their hand in the bag without looking at the object. Can they feel what it is? Increase the number of items in the bag for identification.

Feely bags (alternative method)

You will need smaller bags made out of cotton material roughly 15 cm. square. A draw string is ideal.

Collect a number of small everyday items, ensuring that they are unbreakable, blunt and in common use.

Place one item in each bag. Number the bag, recording the contents and number of the bag on the checklist.

Tie the drawstring or staple the end of the bag, (taking care there are no lose staples to catch on patients' fingers).

Give each member of the group a bag to prod and feel. Can they identify the contents?

Pass bags around the group until everyone has felt all the bags.

This activity can be used as stimulation, to encourage response and give interest. Staff can hint, prompt and ask questions to raise awareness and thinking. The drawstrings can easily be undone to show what was in the bag.

This activity can be run as a quiz.

Patients can give their 'guess' to staff members to write down and score or individuals can have paper and pencil to note their own answers.

The winner has the greatest number of correct items. Make this activity more difficult by adding to the number of items used and the complexity of the task of guessing. Use less frequently encountered items or small objects.

2.   **Sock Scavenge**

You will need some big socks or bags for this game and a few small everyday items to put inside. Make sure each sock has identical contents, e.g. pencil, spoon, apple, coin.

Each patient is given a sock which they should not look into.

The leader asks for an item from the sock and sees who can produce it first by feeling around in their sock.

3.   **What is it?**

Collect everyday objects — unbreakable, not too sharp or too large.

With the group in a circle give one person an object to hold behind their back. They must keep it behind them and not look at it, just feel it with your help. Encourage them to describe to the group what they feel and guess what it is.

'It's round and smooth'

If necessary prompt by asking questions. *'What is it made of?'*

With less confused patients you may use a scarf as a blindfold but some patients will object to this and it could cause worry and confusion. Check with your group first.

4.   **How does it feel?**

Instead of objects for this, you need samples or scraps of materials.

Collect items with specific tactile qualities, e.g.

glass paper, steel wool, feathers, sponge, fir cone, wood shavings, velvet, brush, wool, paper, seaweed, metal, cotton wool.

You may simply pass these round singly on a tray, encourage feeling, stroking, prodding and commenting.

Or pass around, encouraging descriptions:

'How would you say it feels, Harry?'

'Jane, what is it like to touch?'

If there is little response then fill in the gaps and suggest what patients are feeling as you run their fingers over the sample.

'This is rough and scratchy, isn't it?'

'Just feel how cold and smooth this is.'

SMELL

Smells revive memories and have associations for people.

Gather together small pots or jars, preferably of the same size. (Your Pathology Department or Pharmacy may be able to help here. Otherwise try baby food jars or yoghurt pots, although these are really too large.)

Also gather together a selection of products with distinctive smells. Here are some suggestions:

onions, curry powder, lavender, orange, soap, horse linament, lemons, disinfectant, ginger, garlic, boiled eggs, eucalyptus, cloves, mint, beer, peppermint essence, tobacco.

If you have transparent jars, cover the sides with self-adhesive labels or paint the pots so that samples can not be seen. Put a small sample in each pot and cover with a little cotton wool. With fluids soak the cotton wool.

With a less able group you may like to make up a set of enough pots to give each person their own sample of each ingredient to study with the help of a staff member. Keep lids of cling film on the pots to retain the scent. Prepare the pots as near to the time of using as possible or 'top up' nearer the time. Do not leave them to grow mould! (Another group could use the same pots to save preparation time — as long as not to long elapses between usage.)

Number the pots and write down what they are for quick reference.

Hand out the pots to your group and invite comment, exchanging pots when conclusions have been reached, join in by hinting, encouraging, agreeing.

Variations:

Let each person smell the same pot in turn then see if the group agrees on its contents.

With a more able group, give each person a paper and pencil to write the number of the pot and what they think is in it before passing it on and receiving the next pot.

Perfumes

Collect samples of perfume, hand lotion, after shave, etc. Let patients try them out and enjoy the smells — encourage sampling and comments.

SIGHT

Posters or Pictures

With early groups when trying to stimulate, focus attention and encourage response, it might be helpful to use a picture.

Choose a large, colourful and detailed picture or poster which can be put up on a board in front of the group and easily seen.

Talk about what is happening in the scene depicted, where it might be, what time of the year it is (according to weather or plants) or the way the people are dressed. Try to involve patients in your talk by inviting comment or asking questions.

'It looks a bit cloudy, do you think it's winter time Bert?'

'She's wearing a blouse the same colour as your dress Amy!'

'Would you like to go there, Frank?'

'How many people are there, John?'

At first patients will not be sure what is expected but if you find a selection of posters or pictures and repeat this activity they will learn how to respond. Be prepared to do most of the work yourself to start with and be content to have gained the attention of your group and stimulate them if only briefly at the beginning.

Consider using:

—   travel posters showing scenes from England or abroad

—   copies of paintings by Brueghel

—   Home Safety Poster

Particularly useful for Day patients

—   Road Safety Posters

Mount displays using books left open at colourful pages as well as posters. Leave patients free to explore or see if their attention is taken by any of the material, or draw attention to the display, point out details of posters and pass round books commenting, questioning and seeing who shows a particular interest. You will be adding to the variety of stimuli you offer your patients both visually and verbally and you may be able to include touching and handling of any samples or exhibits you have found to add to the theme.

Remember that there may be records or tape recordings that go with your material, bird songs, train sounds, etc.

You may be able to borrow books from the library, even collected for you if you explain what you want. For example, a range of books on trains, gardens, birds, cats, hobbies or countries. (Some libraries may consider giving your hospital condemned, much used library picture books which they have taken out of circulation). You might find posters from organisations, travel firms or companies or education suppliers which give more pictures and interest for these themes.

Colour

Ensure that the brightness, stimulation and attraction of colour are available to your patients in the R.O. room.

Remark on and draw attention to colour when talking to your group. Use coloured, rather than plain, cards and objects for activities.

Make your patients even more aware of colour with the following simple game:—

Recognition of colour

You will need cards plainly painted with basic colours or covered with colour cut from pictures in magazines, etc. They should be at least 10 cm. square.

1. Hold up the colour cards in turn, asking or naming the colour according to the capabilities of the group. How many other objects of that colour can be seen in the room?

2. Use flash cards with the names of colours. Hold up the colour card and flash card simultaneously.

3.   With patients sitting around the table, picture cards and flash cards spread on the table for matching. Encourage and help patients match picture card to flash card talking as you go and pointing out items of that colour.

4.   Use a 5 cm. wooden dice painted on each face with a different colour.

Patients sit around table and throw dice in turn. Thrower recognises and calls the colour he has thrown. Staff keep a record. First person to throw each colour wins.

5.   As above but this time patient must name an object that is the same colour as the one thrown on the dice.
(Make sure there are plenty of coloured items in the room to act as clues.)

6.   **Associations**

Often patients will retain rhymes and similies in their minds when other information is gone. They can be encouraged and pleased by their success if those things can be brought out. Give a lead in and see if they can finish the simili:

As green as . . . . **grass**
As white as . . . . **snow**
As black as . . . . **soot**
As red as a. . . . . **beetroot**
As brown as a . . . . **berry**
As yellow as a . . . . **buttercup**
As blue as the . . . . **sky**

7.   **Colour Quiz**

Make up questions which require a colour to form the answer. (Commercial quiz books may help here.)

The Union Jack is coloured. . . . . **red, white and blue**
The colour for danger is . . . . **red**
Something borrowed, something. . . . . **blue**
The colours of traffic lights are . . . . **red, amber, green**

A royal colour is	**purple**
Green can be made from	**yellow and blue**
When you are well and happy, you are feeling in the	**pink**
Rudolf the reindeer had a . . . . nose	**red**
Bing Crosby sang. . . . . .Christmas	**White**
The . . . . Bells of Scotland	**blue**
You go . . . . with the cold	**blue**
You go . . . . .with envy	**green**
You go . . . . with rage	**purple**
My love is like a. . . . . rose	**red**
Name two birds with colour in their names	**Bluetit**
	Yellow hammer
	Goldfinch
	Greenfinch
	Blackbird
Name two towns or cities with colours in their names	**Blackpool**
	Redhill
	Greenford
	Blackburn

HEARING

Aural stimulation is readily available to your patients. They hear you talking to them in Classroom sessions. They hear the responses of fellow patients, conversations, the radio, TV, etc. However, this form of stimulation can be varied by using specially made tape recordings or commercially available records and tapes of sounds such as bird calls, train noises and other sound effects.

When planning your sessions give consideration to any sounds which could complement the material you are using. For long-stay patients in particular there may be familiar noises which once played a great part in their lives. The reintroduction of these sounds may stimulate and arouse interest where other material has failed. Use your knowledge of patients' backgrounds when thinking along these lines. While in hospital patients are cut off from many everyday noises which they could be helped to keep in touch with.

Make up a tape of various sounds which could be listened to and discussed or used for a quiz. Here are some suggestions —

various animal noises, horses' hooves, waterfalls, church bells, market day sounds, traffic, machinery, buses, shop tills, children's playgrounds, factory whistles, pelican crossing, ambulance, police car, kettle boiling, crockery sounds, the vacuum cleaner, light being switched on, car horn.

A tape like this could be used on many occasions and with other groups. Harder still, requiring added auditory discrimination would be recordings of voices. These could be of group members, staff, other patients and visitors to the ward known by all the group, e.g. chaplain and voluntary workers.

Music

Songs are often remembered when other forms of speech are forgotten and therefore periods when active participation in singing is happily possible can be a great relief and joy to many patients.

For those who enjoy a sing-song, it can act as a reward for the 'hard work' part of the session. It will add to the relaxed atmosphere and provide added stimulation.

Those who do not sing may clap or tap with the music and still feel involved.

Consider the use of simple percussion instruments, some of which could be easily and cheaply made with the help of the patient. These could be used to accompany records although a piano or other musical lead makes all the difference.

Remember to record some of the efforts to play back for fun.

Find out which songs your patients know by playing records or tapes and talking about singers. Older patients always seem to enoy the songs of the war years or pub songs and patriotic songs and hymns are often very popular.

You can prepare blackboards or flip-charts with clearly printed words of songs. Or duplicated song sheets could be passed round. (These are not vital because people usually sing for enjoyment from memory, but if you want to use this activity a lot, it will help patients to read and learn if they have a sheet in front of them.)

A piano is a boon — if you are, or have, a pianist! If not, perhaps a friend could be persuaded to make a tape recording of the accompaniment for a selection of the patient's favourite songs.

Otherwise, there are sing-a-long records, e.g. Max Bygraves, Russ Conway, Mrs Mills.

This favourite music could be used in the background while doing simple exercises but beware of it as a distraction, overcoming the benefit of its stimulation. (See Physical Exercise.)

Song games

Have a list at hand to help prompt or hint at titles for those who get stuck.

Who can think of a song with a:—

- — Girl's name in it?
- — Boy's name in it?
- — Flower mentioned in it?
- — Place mentioned in it?

    —   Colour mentioned in it?

    —   Song sung by famous singer . . . .

    —   Which songs came from the show . . . . . . (or vice versa)

These questions can be answered spontaneously by the group or by patients in turn. Or they can be answered by the song being sung and followed as quickly as possible by a further song on the same theme until the group runs out.

One Finger One Thumb Keep Moving

Who is the singer?

Play snippets of records or make up a tape for this purpose. Ask who the singer is.

Play familiar songs and patients will often enjoy joining in as well as remembering who the original artist is.

What is the music?

Play pieces of relatively well-known classical music or band playing well-known songs to be identified.

A group which really enjoys music may be encouraged to hum, tap out, whistle or in some way produce a well-known tune without words for another group to guess.

Alternatively you could give them a title from a prepared list of songs and let them take turns to perform and guess. Be prepared to embellish less recognisable renditions by joining in. Try:

Rule Britania, Hokey Cokey, I do like to be beside the seaside, Tipperary.

It's good to end a session with music because it usually 'lifts' and stimulates the group and leaves them feeling happy.

Songs with Places Mentioned

1) Yellow Rose of Texas

2) I left my Heart in San Francisco

3) Slow boat to China

4) Londonderry Air

5) Galway Bay

6) Maybe it's because I'm a Londoner

7) Men of Harlech

8) White cliffs of Dover

9) Rose of Tralee

10) April in Paris

11) Tulips from Amsterdam

12) Paris in the Springtime

13) Tipperary

14) Flower of Scotland

15) London bridge is falling down

16) The day we went to Bangor

17) I belong to Glasgow

18) The road to Mandalay

19) Ye banks and braes o' bonnie Doon

20) Bluebell of Scotland

21) London town

22) In Dublin's fair city

23) Georgia

24) Chicago

25) Wales, Wales

26) Skye boat song

Songs with colours in them

e.g. Red, Red Robin *and* White Christmas

1)   Ruby

2)   Blue Jeans

3)   Blue Suede Shoes

4)   Green, Green Grass

5)   White Cliffs of Dover

6)   White Christmas

7)   Mellow, Yellow

8)   Paint it Black

9)   Yellow Rose of Texas

10) Yellow Submarine

11) Bye, Bye Blackbird

12) Red Room

13) Blue Skies

14) Blue Danube

15) Black Night

16) Black Velvet Band

17) Red Sails in the Sunset

18) Whiter Shade of Pale

19) Brown Sugar

20) Little Brown Jug

21) My Love is like a Red, Red Rose

22) Yellow Brick Road

23) That Olde Black Magic

24) Tie a Yellow Ribbon

26) Bluc Moon

27) There is a green hill far away

28) Red Roses for a Blue Lady

29) Two Little Girls in Blue

30) Rudolf the Red-Nosed Reindeer

31) There'll be blue birds

32) Oranges and Lemons

33) Little Green Apples

34) Jeanie with the Light Brown Hair

35) Brown Girl in the Ring

36) Little Grey Home in the West

37) Two Eyes of Blue

38) Lilac Wine

39) Maid with Nut Brown Hair

40) Golden Earings

41) Lavender's Blue

42) Black is Black

43) Little White Bull

44) Rhapsody in Blue

45) Blue Ridge Mountains

46) My Blue Heaven

47) Gold and Silver Waltz

48) Ten Green Bottles

49) Silver Threads Among the Gold

50) Lily the Pink

Songs with Names Mentioned

1) Annie Laurie
2) Barbara Ann
3) Bobbie Shaftoe
4) Delilah
5) Daisy
6) Frankie and Johnny
7) Gigi
8) Goodnight Irene
9) Jeanie with the light brown hair
10) Katie
11) I'll take you home again Kathleen
12) John Peel
13) John Brown's Body
14) When Johnnie comes marching home
15) Lily Marlene
16) Molly Malone
17) Maria
18) Nellie Dean
19) Ophelia
20) Polly, Wolly Doodle
21) Rose Marie
22) Sally
23) Tammy
24) Tom Cobbley

Songs with Flowers Mentioned

1) Apple Blossom Time
2) We'll Gather Lilacs
3) Tiptoe through the Tulips
4) My love is like a Red, Red Rose
5) Roses of Picardy
6) The Bonnie Heather
7) Don't Eat the Daises
8) Eidelweiss
9) The Blue Bells of Scotland
10) Lavenders Blue

4 Practical Activities

Occasional brief periods of practical activity as part of a session may help in several ways. They provide the opportunity for natural use of equipment, such as scissors and kitchen utensils; for following instructions and achieving results which are both useful to others and give pleasure and confidence to the maker.

Note: You must be very well organised with equipment, samples, materials, to hand so that you do not risk losing patients' interest and attention while you delay the meeting getting ready for the activity. It may help to layout everything on trays ready to be placed on the table at the right moment and then taken away more easily when you are ready to move on to the next part of the session.

Suggested Tasks

1. **Picture Cards**

    Go through magazines selecting pictures to be used in making up visual aids. Give subjects to be searched for, write them up on the board and possibly attach a few samples as a guide. Move around the group reminding, pointing out, encouraging and adding comments or questions to keep attention focused.

    Look for pictures of:

    flowers, people, furniture, houses, animals, food, crockery, birds, etc

    Pictures should be torn out of magazines by tearing out the full page and collected into marked folders or envelopes. They can be carefully cut out and mounted on card or salvaged cereal or other boxes.

    Patients could help stick the pictures on the card. You may like to cover them with transparent adhesive plastic to make them more durable and wipeable. Either print, lettraset or cut out print from magazines to make labels to mount on card in the same way as the pictures. Number or letter the cards for reference and to put them in order for quizzes.

2.   **Simple sewing**

Make bags for the 'Feely Game' (see page 113).

Make up bean bags to use in place of balls in some of the active games.

Make fabric dice. (Patients may be able to tack or backstitch these.)

Other projects could include:—

(a)   Making up and painting the boxes for active games (see Active Games page 142).

(b)   Making simple percussion instruments for music sessions.

(c)   Making cards or decorations for festive occasions.

(d)   Adding to information about the date or season, e.g.

'It's George's birthday — We made him a card.'

'We're making decorations for Christmas.'

'We arranged spring flowers.'

(e)   Making cards or small gifts for relatives.

Useful activities such as sewing on buttons and simple mending may help encourage clothes consciousness and smartness. If this is done once or twice in sessions it could possible be carried on out of therapy time.

3.   **Cooking**

To use any sort of cooking activity you will need to have made very careful preparations indeed. Utensils and ingredients need to be put out for each person and you will need a high staff/patient ratio to cope with confused and disorientated patients both safely and with satisfactory results. Remember to ensure that you have dealt with cooking utensils and ingredients in Object Recognition before you move on to attempt any food preparation. Staff will have a lot of clearing up to do!

However, if you feel that the introduction of this homely practical activity will stimulate and interest as well as prove worthwhile, it will certainly be enjoyed.

To tie in with your R.O. programme, it is best if patients use their regular familiar room and the materials are brought in for them. A much more advanced group may enjoy occasional use of the kitchen or one person could help move to and fro with staff getting things into and out of the oven but on the whole this is best done outside the R.O. session.

Choose very simple projects. Write up instructions on the board and go through them. Give each patient a tray with what they need on it. (Bring in a bowl, soap and towels for handwashing if you do not have a sink in the room).

Distribute aprons. Consider using plastic or paper covers (disposable sheets?) for tables.

Demonstrate to and instruct each patient individually.

Suggestions for cooking

(a)   Without using an oven:

- sandwiches

- jellies, trifles and fillings for flans set in jelly or gelatine (you will need an electric kettle).

- savoury toppings for cracker biscuits

- salads

- pickling e.g. onions, red cabbage

As the group progresses and is more capable move on to easy recipes,

(b)   Using an oven or slow cooker:

- biscuits, buns, shortcake, jam tarts. (Prepare beforehand careful step-by-step instructions for these, making sure you know the timing of each recipe.)

— stew or soup. Vegetables and meat could be prepared and possibly cooked in the room using a slow cooker or in the kitchen after the session has finished.

The group could possibly work together to provide a small party for another group of patients or a group member's birthday. Food could be made over a period of time and stored in tins and/or a helpful member of staff's freezer. A variety of foods such as shortbread, gingerbread, cakes, tarts and flans could be made and stored. In this way stocks could gradually be built up and the group would not need to work exclusively on cooking before the party.

Group members would enjoy the praise and pleasure of both other patients and staff who shared the party with them.

A group of more able patients and particularly Day patients could be helped by discussing the ingredients used in a cooking session.

'What do we need to make shortcake?'

'What quantity would you suggest?'

Encourage them to think about these things. Remind them or help them work out the answer or look it up.

Focus on utensils, oven temperature and any safety procedures. Ask about costs. Let each person make out a shopping list and give prices they think appropriate. Alternatively you can give each person a copy of the same shopping list which they then supply prices for. Discuss and compare results with the list you have previously compiled.

Produce packets of the necessary ingredients with prices marked on them from your shopping bag. Let patients look and see if they were right. Allow conversation and comments to flow on the subject of rising costs, housekeeping, budgeting, shopping problems, pensions, etc.

Make a note of any subject causing most interest or concern which you could develop at a later date or on which you could prepare helpful information or a useful activity.

5 Physical Activities

EXERCISES

Physical exercise can often stimulate your patients more than words. It will help them to become more awake alert and receptive. It can be accompanied by music for added stimulation and can give enjoyment too.

It is, therefore, well worth considering the addition of some form of physical exercise in your programme.

1. You may consider using some action words which give extra vitality to the physical response, aid learning and increase stimulation. Words such as:

    up, down, clap, mix/stir (as in cooking), push, roll (as in pastry), kick, stamp, left, right

    spoken or shouted out by the group to the accompaniment of the appropriate action should cause response. Encourage patients to join in with you, doing each movement several times as they call or shout the word.

2. Games such as 'Simon Says' can be adapted to the name of the leader and will test the concentration of a more able group.

    'Simon says do this' (demonstrate an action)

    'Simon says do that' (demonstrate an action)

    But if the words 'Simon Says' are missed out and a command given *'Do this'*, or *'Do that'* the group should not follow the action. They should only react to what Simon says.

3. Simple actions could be initiated by the leader then patients encouraged to follow without instruction i.e. just by watching and copying. Speeded up they test out attention, concentration, agility and co-ordination,

    e.g. arms up/down

    feet up/down

    shoulders up/down

    arms in front, then up, clap, down

    knees up

4. Try giving instruction without demonstration so that patients need to really listen and take in what you are saying. Work on their knowledge of left and right,

    e.g. left/right arm down

    left/right leg up

    touch left knee

    tap left shoulder

5. Exercises using movements involved in everyday activities will encourage independence.

    Mime the action and help patients to follow:

    e.g. *putting on vest, undoing back of fastening, pulling on socks, combing back of hair.*

    Identify the movements needed for each activity and plan a programme working up to them. Give instruction and demonstration as usual.

    e.g. back of neck

    arms up, bend elbows

    hands together on head

    slide hands down back of head as far as you can go

6. Exercises done in time to music are particularly stimulating. Many patients will enjoy the rhythm and gain satisfaction from following the pattern of the music. They will often sing-a-long too and enjoy themselves. Choose songs from the war years for older patients or pub songs. Listen to records and work out movements to go with them. Some clapping and foot tapping can be included.

7. 'Hokey Cokey' is often a remembered favourite and can be done sitting down. A lively combination of music, singing and action – an enjoyable way to end the session.

ACTIVE GAMES

With these games you can stimulate your patients and encourage co-ordination and improve muscle tone while providing enjoyment. Active participation will assure you of patients' attention and concentration. Scoring these games will help in their awareness of number. The different equipment used adds to variety and stimulation.

You can easily make the equipment for some of the following games by using large cardboard boxes. You will need a craft or other sharp knife and good coloured paints. The results will not stand a tremendous amount of wear and tear but can be replaced easily and cheaply. (Perhaps someone in your O.T. Department can help out with something wooden and more substantial. They could well come up with further ideas, too.)

1(a) Indoor Golf (Simple Version)

Requirements: golf sized balls
walking-stick or rolled newspaper
cardboard box with two opposite sides removed (see page 142)
blackboard and chalk

Instructions:

(i) Patients should be encouraged to stand for this game but it can be played sitting, if necessary.

(ii) The starting line is marked and the box placed at the far end of the room. (It can be placed nearer the patient if greater difficulty is encountered. If patients remain seated, then staff move the box opposite the patient whose turn it is.)

(iii) Each patient in turn goes to the starting line and using the walking-stick upside down as a golf club drives the ball into the box.

(iv) Each patient has two to four balls.

(v) The game should be scored on a blackboard.

(vi) The highest scorer after a set number of turns wins.

1(b) Indoor Golf (Variation)

Requirements: As for 1(a)

Instructions:

> As in 1(a) but make the target box more difficult with different holes to aim for (see p.142).

2   Skittles

Requirements: 6—12 skittles. (These can be made from cleaned out detergent bottles, painted or varnished, part filled with sand or water to give them weight.)
2 tennis sized balls

Instructions:

(i)   Patients can sit or stand for this game.

(ii) The starting line is marked and the skittles set up at the far end of the room.

(iii) Patients take it in turn to roll the balls and see how many skittles can be knocked down; or patients kick the balls (this is safer when sitting down) and see how many skittles are knocked down.

3   Indoor Football

Requirements: 1 large ball

Instructions:

(i)   Patients sit in a circle and a large ball is rolled into the group.

(ii) Patients kick the ball away from their chairs and try to get it out of the circle by kicking it under the chair opposite them; or mark one chair as a goal and appoint a goal-keeper. Patients should try to kick the ball under the 'goal' chair. The 'goalie' kicks it back into the circle to prevent scoring.

4   **Indoor Netball**

Requirements: 1 child's fishing net with wire head bent over to a perpendicular position, or a home-made equivalent (see p.142)

2 light sponge or air balls

Instructions:

(i)   Patients sit in a circle.

(ii)   Staff move around the group holding the net in front of each patient at about head height.

(iii) Each patient has two balls to try and score in the net.

5   **Target Ball**

Requirements: Tennis sized sponge or air balls

Box with various sized holes cut out of it, (see p.142)

Instructions:

(i)   The game can be played sitting or standing.

(ii)   Mark a starter line (if standing) or place box in middle of group, if sitting.

(iii) Each person in turn throws two — four balls aiming for the smallest holes for highest score.

Indoor Golf — Simple Version

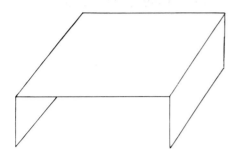

Indoor Golf — Variation

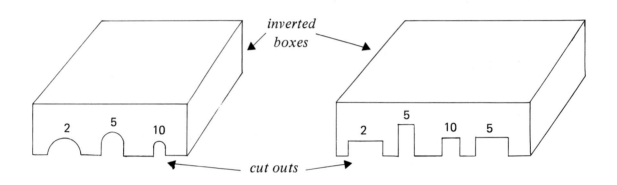

inverted
boxes

cut outs

Indoor Net Ball

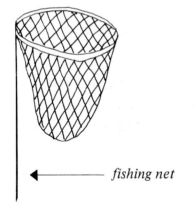

fishing net

Target ball

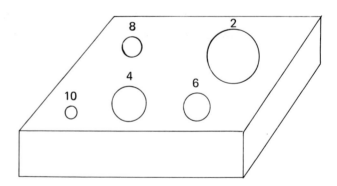

6 Memory Games

Advanced groups may enjoy these games and simple adapted versions can be introduced to encourage efforts from those less able. Some of these games will be too hard for many of your patients.

1   **Memory Tray**

Requirements:

> A few common everyday objects, e.g. cup, toothbrush, sock, apple, book. (Smaller objects, e.g. coins, hairgrips, keys, safety pins can be used when patients are familiar with the game.)
>
> a tray
>
> a tea towel or piece of cloth

Instructions:

> (i)   Place the items on a tray (initially use just two or three items then increase to as many as 20 if your group can cope).
>
> (ii)   Place the items in front of the patients and encourage them to study what is there. Hold up each item in turn and talk about it to help focus attention. Go through all the items at the end.
>
> (iii) When you have done your best to focus attention, cover the tray over with a tea towel or piece of cloth.
>
> (iv)   Ask how many items can be remembered. Either ask each person in turn for an item or let those who remember speak spontaneously. Give clues for those items which no-one can remember. Alternatively give out pencils and paper for each patient to provide their own list.

2   **Memory Bag**

Requirements:

Feely bag (see section on 'Touch' p.113)

Items which will fit in to the bag.

Instructions:

(i)   Items are placed in the bag.

(ii)   The bag is passed around the group and patients feel in the bag trying to identify the objects (without mentioning what they can feel).

(iii) Patients then write down what they can remember feeling.

3   **I packed my bag**

Traditionally this game is played by a group of people giving in turn the name of an appropriate item to be packed in a fictitious bag, probably to go off on holiday. As each item is added, the list of previous items mentioned has to be remembered and repeated.

You will need (for simple version)

Picture cards of clothing/objects; or

Actual articles of clothing/objects

Instructions (Simple Version)

(i)   Hand round the picture cards of clothing or the objects.

(ii)   Start off the group with an item, showing the card/object to the group to aid memory.

(iii) The first person then repeats your item and adds his/her own.

(iv)   Continue round the group, each patient repeating those items which have been mentioned before and then adding their own.

(Patients use the card or actual object as a prompt.)

Note: Bear in mind that the first people to take their turn have less to remember so put people in the order you think best before the start. Consider using staff at the beginning to set the group off on the right track or at the end to take the brunt of remembering.

As you play the simple version collect the items in a bag or on a tray.

(i) When all the items have been collected ask what was put in the bag. Who can remember?

or, when all are collected ask each patient in turn to remember their item, retrieve and name it.

or, when all are collected proceed to play the game in its original form, prompting or holding up appropriate items to remind patients and ensure flow.

Instructions (Traditional Version)

The traditional game is done verbally thus:

1st person: I packed my bag and in it I put my pyjamas.

2nd person: I packed my bag and in it I put my pyjamas and perfume.

3rd person: I packed my bag and in it I put my pyjamas, perfume and bikini.

There are invariably a few hilarious items that get added!

Variations (make them seasonal, topical)

(a) I made a stew and in it I put ....

(b) I had a party and invited .... (people from the whole group)

(c) I emptied my Christmas stocking and in it I found ....

(d) I went on a journey and called in at .... (use local places).

4 Pelmanism

Requirements:

2 identical sets of picture cards or number cards

2 suits of playing cards, e.g. spades and diamonds.

Instructions:

   (i)   Select a few pairs of cards.

   (ii)   Mix these cards up and place face down on the table.

   (iii) Each person turns over two cards in order to try and find a pair.

   (iv)   If a pair is found, they are removed and stacked beside the person who found them.

   (v)   If odd cards are turned up, the cards are left in their places face up for a while, giving people a chance to remember what they are and where they are. They are then turned back and left in the same position.

   (vi)   The next person turns over a card, leaves it in place and if it matches one already seen, he tries to remember the position of its pair and turns that over. Otherwise he will choose at random hoping to find a match.

   (vii) Play continues until all cards have been paired up.

As concentration is built up so more pairs of cards can be added to the game.

5   **Memory cards**

Requirements:

   Cards with 2 or 3 pictures on them (increasing the number of pictures as patients become more able at the game).

Instructions:

   (i)   Show the card to the patients.

   (ii)   Talk about the pictures.

   (iii) Turn the card over.

   (iv)   Ask what items can be remembered or give patients pencil and paper and let them write down answers; or patients have pencil and card with spaces marked out for them to draw in the pictures they remember.

7 Social Activities

Proverbs and Similes

These are particularly popular with older patients who may be delighted to be reminded of them or find they can remember these early learnt sayings. This will give pleasure as well as confidence. Make a list of collected proverbs and similes (see pp. 155-157) and print them on cards.

1   Read out the first half of a proverb to the group and wait for the second half to be filled in.

   'A stitch in time .... **saves nine.**'

   'Too many cooks .... **spoil the broth.**'

2   Give out cards with the first half written on and see if the end can be supplied by the holder of the card.

3   Hold up the card without speaking and see if the correct ending is forthcoming. A group capable of this could be given a duplicated sheet with the second half left blank to fill in for themselves.

4   Ask patients to supply proverbs and see how many are known. In fact, do this first to help start your collection!

5   Make up clues for proverbs and similes by cutting out pictures or making drawings to illustrate them. Put each clue on a different card to hold up or pass round. If you can draw, then put them on the blackboard in turn.

6   **Pairs and Opposites**

   Give the first name and see who can supply the second, e.g. Cain and Abel. (see pp. 158-161).

7   **People Puzzles**

   For this you will need large pictures of individual people. Full length, standing figures are best. They do not need to be known characters.

   The pictures should be mounted on card and can be covered with self-adhesive transparent plastic to make them more durable.

Each picture is cut into 3, 4 or more pieces to make a very simple jigsaw. Recognisable parts of the body should be separated, i.e. cut off head, arms, trunk, legs and feet.

Keep each puzzle in a separate envelope marked with the number of pieces.

(a) Put puzzle pieces from one envelope out on the table in front of patients. Encourage examination of the pieces and discussion of what part of the body is shown on each piece. Help assemble the pieces by asking for them in turn.

(b) Each patient may be given their own puzzle to assemble.

(c) Puzzles can be made more complicated by cutting pictures into less easily recognisable and smaller pieces.

A small prize can be given for the first person to successfully complete their puzzle.

8 Card Puzzles

Collect Christmas, Easter, Valentine and birthday cards, also post-cards.

Use the cards according to the season.

Cut the cards into a number of easily shaped pieces to make simple puzzles.

Keep the puzzles in separate envelopes and indicate season and number of pieces or degree of difficulty of the puzzles.

Distribute the puzzles to each of the members of your group. Whoever can complete their puzzle first and tell you about the picture wins.

9 Beetle

A dice is thrown in turn around the group.

A 6 must be thrown before the Beetle can be started. The 6 scores a body.

The dice goes on being thrown in turn and parts of the Beetle are added accordingly:

5 for a head	2 for each of the 2 feelers
4 for a tail	1 for each of the 2 eyes
3 for each of the 6 legs	

Patients can draw their Beetles as they go, following the pattern on the right. Otherwise a member of staff can draw a Beetle on the blackboard using the scores of all the group.

A variation would be to make up large Beetles from plywood or cardboard; colour them and mark the number you must throw to earn them and cut up the segments.

Patients can either sit in a circle and play Beetle as a group, throwing a large dice and having a Beetle made up for them. Or, each patient can make up their own Beetle with pieces claimed from a member of staff when they have thrown the dice.

10   Flounders

This game can be simplified and played as a group by using large wooden or card flounders and dice.

Patients sit in a circle and throw a dice. A 1 must be thrown to commence play in earnest. A 1 earns a head

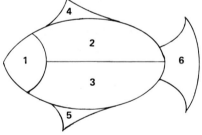

2 and 3 are halves of the body

4 and 5 are fins

6 is a tail

The dice is thrown in turn until a flounder has been formed.

Alternatively, patients may form their own flounder as above.

More able patients will be capable of playing this game in its original, commercial form. Using a collection of flounders throwing 2 dice at a time and forming as many flounders as they can.

11 **Bingo**

This game can be played in its original form using commercially available equipment. However, you should bear in mind that to play with numbers 1–100 could take so long that patients may not be able to maintain concentration and interest. Also, many cards are not sufficiently large or clear for those with poor sight. The amount of numbers to listen out for is too great for anyone who is unused to the game or has poor memory and concentration.

There are some simple versions of the game.

(a) **Card Bingo**

Use 2 identical packs of playing cards.

(i) Distribute the cards from one of the packs giving each patient 2, 3 or 4 according to their ability.

(The cards should be placed face up in front of each patient.)

(ii) Using the second pack of cards, go through them calling out and holding up each one in turn.

(iii) If a patient has the card which is called, then he turns his over, face down or gives it to a member of staff.

(iv) The first person to turn over or hand in all their cards is the winner.

Variations – Make up your own packs of cards using pictures or illustrations mounted on card. Have 2 identical sets of cards showing animals, flowers, famous people, etc. The game is played as above.

(b) **Set Bingo**

Make up Bingo cards by using pictures or illustrations of items normally grouped together for specific purposes. Cards could include such things as:

tea making materials, clothing, meal times.

For each game you would need to collect pictures of the different items needed for or associated with the subject,

e.g. tea making – kettle, teapot, milk bottle, sugar, cup, saucer,
packet of tea/tea bags, teaspoon.

One set of pictures is mounted on individual cards and the other set arranged on large cards in groups of 2 or 3 or 4 according to the ability of your group. Each of the large cards must bear a different combination of pictures of associated objects.

PROVERBS & SAYINGS

1) Make hay .... while the sun shines

2) Look before .... you leap

3) All work and no play .... makes Jack a dull boy

4) A stitch in time .... saves nine

5) Many hands...................................... make light work

6) Too many cooks .... spoil the broth

7) Every cloud...................................... has a silver lining

8) Don't count your chickens .... before they're hatched

9) The early bird .... catches the worm

10) A bird in the hand............................. is worth two in the bush

11) People who live in glass houses............ shouldn't throw stones

12) The leopard can't .... change his spots

13) Let sleeping dogs .... lie

14) Once bitten .... twice shy

15) It's no use crying .... over spilt milk

16) A watched pot .... never boils

17) The grass is always .... greener on the other side

18) The night is always darkest .... just before the dawn

19) Great oaks .... from little acorns grow

20) It's no use keeping a dog .... and barking yourself

21) All that glitters .... is not gold

22) Don't put all your eggs .... in one basket

23) A cat may look .... at a king

24) If you've made your bed .... you must lie on it

25) Half a loaf .... is better than no bread

26) Jack of all trades .... master of none

27) While the cat's away .... the mice will play

28) He who hesitates .... is lost

29) Still waters .... run deep

30) A rolling stone .... gathers no moss

31) You can take a horse to water .... but you can't make him drink

32) It's no good bolting the stable door .... after the horse has gone

33) You can't teach your grandmother ..... to suck eggs

34) Blood is .... thicker than water

35) One rotten apple .... can spoil the barrel

36) There's many a slip twixt .... the cup and the lip

37) It's an ill wind that.............................. blows no good

38) Money is the root................................ of all evil

39) A nod is as .... good as a wink

40) A change is as .... good as a rest

41) A new broom .... sweeps clean

42) Two heads are .... better than one

43) It never rains .... but it pours

44) Better to be safe................................. than sorry

45) Where there's a will .... there's a way

46) He who laughs last .... laughs the longest

SIMILES

1) As light .... **as a feather**

2) As heavy .... **as lead**

3) As mad .... **as a hatter**

4) As mean .... **as old Nick**

5) As right .... **as ninepence**

6) As quick............ **as a flash**

7) As sharp .... **as a needle**

8) As quiet .... **as a mouse**

9) As rosy............. **as an apple**

10) As sweet .... **as sugar**

11) As big .... **as a house/elephant**

12) As thick............ **as two planks**

13) As black .... **as the ace of spades**

14) As drunk .... **as a lord**

15) As dull .... **as ditchwater**

16) As nice .... **as pie**

17) As pleased .... **as punch**

18) As proud .... **as a peacock**

19) As brave .... **as a lion**

20) As brown .... **as a berry**

21) As happy .... **as a sand-boy**

22) As long............. **as your arm**

23) As deep .... **as the ocean**

24) As sly .... **as a fox**

25) As wise .... **as an owl**

26) As keen .... **as mustard**

27) As bold .... **as brass**

28) As good............ **as gold**

29) As free .... **as the air**

30) As fresh .... **as a daisy**

31) As bright .... **as a button**

32) As clean .... **as a whistle**

33) As right .... **as rain**

34) As deaf .... **as a post**

35) As blind .... **as a bat**

36) As small............ **as a mouse**

BIBLICAL PAIRS

Adam and .... Eve

Cain and .... Abel

Abraham and .... Sarah

Jacob and .... Esau

Samson and .... Delilah

Naomi and .... Ruth

Elijah and .... Elisha

David and .... Goliath

Joseph and .... Mary

James and .... John

Isaac and .... Rebecca

Jonah and .... the whale

Daniel and .... the lion

PAIRS OF PEOPLE

1) Hansel and **Gretal**

2) Dr. Jeykell and **Mr. Hyde**

3) Sherlock Holmes and **Dr. Watson**

4) Prince Charles and **Diana, Princess of Wales**

5) Romeo and **Juliet**

6) Ginger Rogers and **Fred Astaire**

7) Princess Anne and **Captain Mark Philips**

8) Robin Hood and **Maid Marion**

9) Rogers and **Hammerstein**

10) Huckleberry Finn and **Tom Sawyer**

11) Gilbert and **Sullivan**

12) Starsky and **Hutch**

13) Bing Crosby and **Bob Hope**

14) Tom and **Jerry**

15) Bonnie and **Clyde**

16) Pop-Eye and **Olive Oil**

17) Napoleon and **Josephine**

18) Rawicz and **Landaur**

19) Anne Siegler and **Webster Booth**

20) Peter Brough and **Archie Andrews**

21) Caesar and **Cleopatra**

22) Tweedledum and **Tweedledee**

23) Laurel and **Hardy**

24) Flannagan and **Allan**

25) Nelson Eddy and **Jeanete McDonald**

26) Victoria and **Albert**

27) Jack and **Jill**

28) Darby and **Joan**

29) Pearl Carr and **Teddy Johnson**

EVERYDAY PAIRS

Steak and **kidney**

Bangers and **mash**

Fish and **chips**

Black and **white/blue**

Bacon and **eggs**

Salt and **pepper**

Man and **woman**

Husband and **wife**

Son and **daughter**

Aunt and **uncle**

Nephew and **niece**

Grandma and **grandad**

Grand-daughter and **grandson**

Brother and **sister**

Table and **chair**

Knife and **fork**

Bread and **butter**

Horse and **cart**

Strawberries and **cream**

Oranges and **lemons**

North and **south**

East and **west**

Fox and **hound**

Mummy and **daddy**

Ceiling and **floor**

Door and **window**

King and **queen**

Dustpan and **brush**

Cup and **saucer**

Birds and **bees**

Sugar and **spice**

Needle and **thread**

Bricks and **mortar**

Toothbrush and **toothpaste**

Moon and **stars**

Socks and **shoes**

Fingers and **thumbs**

Hands and **feet**

Arms and **legs**

Bat and **ball**

Gas and **electricity**

Hat and **coat**

Snakes and **ladders**

Girl and **boy**

Prince and **princess**

OPPOSITES

Up	**Down**	Find	**Lose**
In	**Out**	Near	**Far**
Coming	**Going**	Sad	**Happy**
Back	**Front**	Male	**Female**
Inside	**Outside**	Young	**Old**
Hot	**Cold**	New	**Old**
Heavy	**Light**	True	**False**
Thick	**Thin**	Beautiful	**Ugly**
Short	**Tall**	Day	**Night**
Big	**Little/Small**	Morning	**Afternoon**
Right	**Left/Wrong**	Over	**Under**
Upstairs	**Downstairs**	For	**Against**
Fast	**Slow**	Backwards	**Forwards**
High	**Low**	Push	**Pull**
On	**Off**	Open	**Closed**
Top	**Bottom**	Win	**Lose**
Solid	**Liquid**	Stop	**Go**
Give	**Take**	Tick	**Cross**
Yes	**No**	Autumn	**Spring**
Dry	**Wet**	Weak	**Strong**
Together	**Apart**	Tame	**Wild**
Summer	**Winter**	Rich	**Poor**
Freeze	**Thaw**	a.m.	**p.m.**
First	**Last**		

8 Bibliography

1. FOLSOM J.C. Reality Orientation for the elderly mental patient
    Journal of Geriatric Psychiatry 1968
    1, 291-307

2. BROOK P., DEGUN G., MATHEW M. Reality Orientation, a therapy for Psycho-geriatric Patients: A Controlled Study
    British Journal of Psychiatry 1975
    127, 42-5

2a. WOODS R.T. Reality Orientation and Staff Attention: A Controlled Study
     British Journal of Psychiatry, 1979
     134, 502-7

3. INGLIS J. Psychological practice in geriatric problems
    Journal of Mental Science 1962, *108,* 669-74

4. MEER B., BAKER J.A. Reliability of Measurement of Intellectual functioning of Geriatric Patients
    Journal Gerontology 1965, *20,* 410-14

4a. PATTIE A.H., GILLIARD C.J. A Brief Psychogeriatric Assessment Schedule
     Brit. Journal Psychiatry 1975, *127,* 489-93

5. FISHBACK D.B. Mental Status Questionnaire for Organic Brain Syndrome with a new Visual Counting Test
    Journal Amer. Geriatrics Society 1977, *25,* 167-70

5a. PERKINS L.M. Assessment and Management of Psychogeriatric Patients
     Brit. Journal Occupational Therapy 1982, *45,* 11-14

6. MEER B., BAKER J.A. The Stockton Geriatric Rating Scale
    I. Gerontology 1966, *21,* 393-403

    Creating and Working with small groups in a Psychogeriatric Hospital Ward
    Nursing Times 1981, *77,* 1679-82